HOW PEOPLE GET THEIR POLITICS

Conversations with Americans About the
Experiences that Shaped their Political Beliefs

How People Get Their Politics

Conversations with Americans About the
Experiences that Shaped Their Political Beliefs

Julie Samrick

Published by Motina Books, LLC

How People Get Their Politics
Conversations with Americans About the Experiences that Shaped
Their Political Beliefs

Published by Motina Books, LLC, Van Alstyne, Texas
www.MotinaBooks.com

Library of Congress Control Number: 2020913698
Samrick, Julie
How People Get Their Politics
Conversations with Americans About the Experiences that Shaped
Their Political Beliefs

ISBN-13: 978-1-945060-16-8

For Brian

"Everything can be taken from a man but one thing: the last of the human freedoms- to choose one's attitude in any given set of circumstances."

-   Viktor E. Frankl

CONTENTS

Introduction

On the morning I began writing this introduction, the House Judiciary Committee voted along party lines to approve two articles of impeachment against President Donald Trump. I note the irony because the idea behind writing this book came to me in 2008 when political rancor seemed to be at a boiling point in the United States. By 2020, bitter partisanship is boiling over the sides.

In 2008 I had an epiphany after listening to two acquaintances tell me why they thought their candidate—Barack Obama or John McCain—should be our next president. Their stories were personal, capturing experiences they'd had as children that cemented how they would go on to vote as adults. I sought more of these stories for this book, defining them as "political shaping stories."

I believe that hearing American citizens' political shaping stories could help mend the political divide we are suffering. The more of these stories we hear, the better.

Yet the divide grows deeper. Since 2016, one-third of Americans said they stopped talking to a friend or family member because of politics. The Pew Research Center found that large shares of the population now feel not only frustrated and angry with members of the opposing party, but afraid of them. Fifty-five percent of Democrats said they are fearful of the GOP, while forty-nine percent of Republicans are scared of the Democratic Party.

According to a nationwide survey of college and university students conducted by the Brookings Institution, more than half (fifty-one percent) thought it was "acceptable" to shout down a speaker with whom they disagreed and almost one in five people (nineteen percent) supported using violence to prevent a speaker from delivering an address.

It is no wonder that fewer Americans want to identify with a political party today. While Democratic or Republican Party candidates have won every United States Presidential Election since 1852, and have controlled the United States Congress to some extent since at least 1856, as of October, 2017 Gallup polling found that the majority of Americans identified as Independent at forty-two percent. Thirty-one percent of Americans identified as Democrat and twenty-four percent identified as Republican.

While there have been other times when Americans were deeply divided, there is no other time in the past century when we have been so at odds with one another. Older people I have talked with confirm this. They noted during the interviews included in this book that political parties before the 1960s didn't have the stigmas they do now and whether a candidate identified as a Democrat or a Republican didn't matter as much to voters as a candidate's personality.

It is hard to imagine a time when politicians worked in a bipartisan way. In the 1980s Democratic Speaker of the House Tip O'Neill and Republican President Ronald Reagan regularly had drinks together at the White House. After one partisan fight, O'Neill famously told Reagan, "Old buddy, that's politics—after six o'clock, we can be friends."

Human beings inherently seek communities to which they can belong. Americans may find communities in houses of worship, at workplaces, in schools, and in neighborhoods, to name a few examples. With the advent of both the smart phone and social media at the same time as my epiphany in 2008, it is no wonder more people have sought communities online. Unfortunately, one drawback to not talking to people face-to-face is that our society's discourse has become less personal, and therefore less humane.

Yet in our fast-paced society, a quick assessment to form an opinion has become the new normal. Complicated stories are being reduced to flitting headlines, which are often manipulated to get more views.

It shouldn't be a surprise that the same has happened in our political climate. Though reduced to a single label at times—Democrat or Republican, liberal or conservative—our political identities are really as complex as we are as human beings. To take someone's political identity and whittle it down to a label, we aren't hearing the whole story, and when we dissolve the complexities that tell a full story, we risk a collective losing of our humanity, which is what is currently happening in America.

While working as a journalist I was struck by the realization that everybody has a story. We simply need to listen. In her memoir *Becoming,* former First Lady Michelle Obama talks about many of the passions she prioritized as First Lady, including access to healthcare, social and economic justice, and the power of education, but it was her personal road to caring about those issues, her political shaping story, that I found most fascinating. As a child, Obama's father worked as a precinct captain for Chicago's Democratic Party. At the same time, she was friends with Civil Rights leader Reverend Jesse Jackson's daughter, Santita. Agree with Obama's politics or not, it is clear from the stories in her memoir why she champions the causes that she does.

In her 1993 memoir *The Downing Street Years*, it is evident why England's first female Prime Minister, Margaret Thatcher, was a conservative. She came of age during a recession and cited her father's background as a grocer as the "basis" for her economic philosophy. As she watched her father run his business, Thatcher would turn the experience into a blueprint for her later views on capitalism and global trade. "In effect, I had been equipped at an early age with the ideal mental outlook and tools of analysis for reconstructing an economy ravaged by state socialism," Thatcher wrote.

I sought people from all backgrounds to capture their political shaping stories for this book. Regardless of a person's political beliefs, my only stipulation to booking an interview was that the person is passionate about his or her beliefs. The sixteen political shaping stories that follow reflect people from all ages and backgrounds. They are self-described Democrats, Republicans, and Independents. There are progressives, liberals, and conservatives. The oldest person was born in 1923 and the youngest was born in 1998. By giving first names only my goal was to show the interview subjects as symbols of society at large. Their stories are unique, just like the hundreds of millions of other Americans whose stories also need to be heard.

While I was conscious to not reduce distinctive experiences to one-dimensional stereotypes, the English major in me conjured metaphors to capture each person's experience. These metaphors are used for chapter titles. I also chose to pair interviews in each chapter for the purpose of juxtaposition.

The conversations that follow include stories about how cancer, religion, and war shaped people's politics. A man and a woman each shared their thoughts on being black in America. One man passionately defended his decision not to vaccinate his children. There are powerful immigrant stories from people who were born in Mexico, Poland, and Taiwan. A longtime U.S. State Department employee explained how his view of America was shaped in large part from living abroad. Two public servants shared their opposite, but equally passionate, views of what would be the best policies to move America forward. A World War II veteran and a former child during that war both spoke about the silver linings that came from living during wartime. One month after wrapping this book, the novel coronavirus COVID-19 wreaked havoc on America and the world, shedding some light on what those older Americans said about people uniting during wartime.

During our conversations I did not ask about education, jobs, spouses, or children unless the interview subjects brought up any of those as part of their political shaping stories. Sometimes this led us off track from politics, but I chose to save the full interview so that the full picture of each person is accurate.

I didn't ask interrogating questions because I wanted people to share their authentic stories, without feeling on defense. I asked follow-up questions only when more clarification was needed. Plus, I've always believed that the best questions are the ones that stem from true curiosity. In her book *You're Not Listening* author

Kate Murphy affirmed this stance on questioning when she described how a Harvard Law School professor named Gillien Todd advises students in her negotiations course to be mindful of their own internal beliefs and biases when asking questions. "Your internal stance should be one of curiosity," Todd is known to tell students. I have always believed this as well.

I asked the same questions at the start of every interview, including year of birth, where they were born, where they grew up, who was in their childhood family, and how they label themselves politically, which I wrote exactly as they described to start each section. I also asked each person whether his or her real first name or a pseudonym should be used. In every case but one a person's real name is given.

I prompted each person to think of one or more memories that stood out as shaping their political beliefs. It became clear that a person's politics are shaped by a unique layering of influences and circumstances. If we were born to different parents, or in another decade, or in a different part of the country or the world, we might actually advocate for the same policies as the neighbor who we are at odds with now.

In a few instances a mind was changed later in life, but by and large I found that people's political opinions were formed by the time they reached young adulthood.

Regardless of their beliefs, a dichotomy emerged from these interviews, which explains the conflict we see in the country today. While everyone agreed that we have grown polarized as a nation because of politics, everyone felt just as passionately that their vision for America is the best one.

There are contradictions when comparing the interviews. What one person says would make "a more perfect union," another person believes the exact opposite. While one called the Democratic Party the all-inclusive "big tent," another used the exact term to describe the GOP. While one person argued why we must keep the Electoral College as is, another just as reasonably outlined why she feels it is archaic. While one person recalled a childhood when "everybody loved Jimmy Carter," another person recalled the thirty-ninth President's term in office and how "everybody" disliked him.

I conducted many of the interviews in the latter part of 2019 while the field of Democratic Party candidates ahead of the 2020 Presidential Election was still large, which is why certain candidates who later left the race are brought up. I decided not to cut these sections as I felt doing so would detract from a person's story.

All opinions offered in this book are those of the interview subjects alone. Their exact words are used unless they are precisely paraphrased.

I ultimately learned that political beliefs translate to a person's value system. They are multi-dimensional and core to who many people are. If political identities are so entrenched, then why do we try so hard to change other people's opinions? And what makes us think that we can? Is it arrogance? Is it ignorance? We might as well give up trying because our political beliefs come from pivotal moments and from important figures in our lives. In *You're Not Listening*, Murphy explained a study where neuroscientists discovered that parts of people's brains lit up as if they were being "chased by a bear" when their political beliefs were challenged. "And when we are in this fight, flight, or freeze mode," Murphy writes, "It's incredibly hard to listen."

Still, despite all the noise and different sources trying to persuade people to change their politics, we shake our heads in wonder when the polls, and people's political identities, remain unchanged.

We are a society that promotes inclusiveness and tolerance. We teach our children to value diversity in all its forms. Yet we are brazenly intolerant when it comes to people whose political beliefs differ from our own. While writing this book I felt hopeful as it became clear that we're not as different as we like to believe.

HOW PEOPLE GET THEIR POLITICS

What I hope readers gain by reading this book is the understanding that we are not going to change other people's minds about their political views but we can broaden the discourse. We are more complex than the one-dimensional labels we often hear, including Democrat, Republican, progressive, or libertarian, and the dehumanizing labels that are often attached to a person's political identity.

As children we are told not to discuss politics. But if we're to break bread with people, why not talk about the things that matter most—those things that make a difference in our lives, including healthcare, immigration, or whether more or less gun legislation will make us safer? While you may feel uncomfortable reading certain interviews—some may even trigger you—I challenge you to keep reading.

Our beliefs are subjective, but powerful to the core of who we are. As a society we must listen to one another and seek leaders who can do the same. Until we realize that we are not going to change minds, we will not be able to move this country forward.

My ultimate hope is that this book adds humanity to the conversation.

Julie Samrick
April, 2020

Chapter 1

"Outside the Box"
Patrick

"A World View"
Steve

Patrick
"Outside the Box"

Born—1963 in Atlantic City,
New Jersey
Political Identity—Libertarian

Patrick is proudly beholden to no political party. Just as I thought I could pinpoint his politics, he would evade labeling. Patrick believes the federal government should have a limited role in people's lives but don't call him a Republican. He is furious about climate change, but don't label him a Democrat either. As a form of protest, Patrick stopped voting more than a decade ago, yet he keeps a keen eye on national and global issues. He is consistent when it comes to suspicion of establishment thinking and he holds constant watch over what he deems the chokehold of government interference.

Today the Air Force veteran and father of four lives in Oklahoma with his second wife and their two young children, ages three and five. Patrick and his wife have chosen to homeschool their children and they have also chosen not to vaccinate them. Patrick believes Americans are over-taxed and that both the American public education system and the second amendment are under constant attack.

Patrick's politics are somewhat surprising given his "Bobby Kennedy liberal" beginnings, but if one looks closely, Patrick's skepticism seems to be bred from the harsh realities he experienced as a young child. Born the eighth of ten siblings, Patrick was raised in an Irish Catholic family in Pleasantville, New Jersey. His early childhood memories are not ones of lollipops and naiveté, but set against the backdrop of the Vietnam War, and by the time he was fifteen, the death of his mother.

To back up even further, Patrick was born into a family already in mourning. Among Patrick's earliest memories was the collective grief his family shared over the shock and anguish caused by the assassination of President John F. Kennedy.

"I was an altar boy and went to Catholic school. I grew up knowing that our first Irish Catholic President was assassinated," he explained.

From then "the biggest events" of Patrick's childhood were when Martin Luther King Jr. and then Bobby Kennedy were also assassinated. "It was huge," Patrick recalled. "We were like the true, Bobby Kennedy liberals. It was like someone from our own family had been killed."

It was once he enlisted in the Air Force, and then throughout his young adult life, that Patrick shaped his own political beliefs. He would go on to express his beliefs in a 2013 documentary he created, entitled, "A Patriot in the Making: Raising Our Children to be Aware and Prepared for the Crazy World in Which We Live."

You were a small child during the Vietnam War. What do you remember thinking at that time?

P: My family hated the war. There was no arguing over who was right and who was wrong. It just was. It was normal for somebody in my family to make the comment, "Aw, that stupid war... Pass me the mashed potatoes."

We were really into sports, especially because I had seven brothers. I remember when Mohammad Ali said, "Ain't no Vietnamese ever did anything to me. Why should I go over there and kill them?" We loved (Ali). We thought he was the greatest boxer ever.

We never came across anyone really for the war either. I remember walking up to meet my friends with a peace sign. By the time I was a teenager I was carrying "Save the Whales" signs with my friends to protest nukes.

During Vietnam we saw the protests and the Watts riots on TV. It was all pretty scary back in the day, but where I grew up in Pleasantville there was an even mix of different races and I remember thinking that we all got along just fine. The news media really pushed the black versus white paradigm though.

Do you remember hearing about soldiers dying?

P: I do remember. When I was really young, maybe seven or eight, there was this lady we always saw at church who had a little kid with her. She was real pretty and she wore this blue jacket. My brothers and I would say, "Who's that pretty lady, Mom?"

She'd say, "That lady lost her husband in Vietnam."

What do you remember about the years after the war ended?

P: After Nixon came in and ended the war and (Gerald) Ford took over, I remember going to the Atlantic City Boardwalk with my eighth-grade class and meeting Ford. I got to shake his hand.

At that time, I didn't understand there was a right or a left in politics. There wasn't such a false left/ right dichotomy then. Everyone was mixed, and got along, you know? We didn't really know anything except that my father was always griping about taxes. Everybody liked Jimmy Carter, but I wanted Ford to win the election because I shook his hand. I had a childish impression of who was the better candidate.

Your parents were Democrats?

P: Strangely enough, they were a mix of both. They were fiscally conservative and socially liberal, but not too liberal. Catholics are staunchly pro-life, but for helping the poor and needy. Growing up I wasn't super poor, but we were from the other side of the tracks. We knew what it was like to go hungry and to be cold in the winter…We knew what it was like to have good years and bad years.

Why do you think dichotomies, both with race and political parties, have been created?

P: It's easier to control people if you give them fewer choices. When my kids want something to eat, I say, "Would you rather have this or that? Which one?"

As for the dichotomy in government, I think it's pure psychological propaganda. A lot of people don't understand, but if you read the National Defense Authorization Act, it is now legal for the media and for the government to lie and propagandize when they see fit.

JS: The U.S. Congress oversees the defense budget primarily through two yearly bills, one of which is the National Defense Authorization Act. This bill determines the agencies responsible for defense, establishes funding levels, and sets the policies under which money will be spent. The first NDAA was passed in 1961.

P: People think the Patriot Act is so terrible. "Oh, cops get away with murder, and they hardly get any years in prison if they ever go to prison." Well, that's by design. It's in the Patriot Act.

JS: By definition, the Patriot Act is legislation passed in 2001 to improve the abilities of U.S. law enforcement to detect and deter terrorism.

Three conservative politicians stand out as shaping Patrick's political ideology as a young adult—one in a negative way and in two men Patrick was refreshed to finally find like-mindedness.

P: I couldn't stand Ronald Reagan. I thought he was a war mon-ger with Iran Contra and everything. Then in the 1990s I remember I started listening to some conservatives like Alan Keyes, who seemed so eloquent to me. I'd never really heard the conservative side of things.

JS: Alan Keyes ran for President of the United States in 1996, 2000, and in 2008.

P: Keyes was like a true, staunch, pro-life guy and came up with these amazing speeches. I was like, "Wow! He's pretty interesting." I remember he was running against (Bill) Clinton, and I was in the Air Force.

Tell me about your time in the Air Force. How did that come to be?

P: In 1982 I was nineteen and had nothing to do. I mean, I had a lot to do—I was an artist and a graphic designer since I can remember. I painted a lot of portraits and did a lot of painting, and it came up that I could do painting and graphic design in the Air Force, but I didn't really have any idea of what I wanted to do. I didn't have any knowledge of the world.

I joined to figure what life was about and I chose the Air Force because it's known as the "thinking man's service." It has a harder test to get in. I also didn't want to carry a twenty-five pound pack in the Army or the Marines.

I was stationed at the Fairchild Air Force Base in Spokane, Washington. I already had a portfolio of massive amounts of illustration and design work, so I went direct duty assignment. My job was to paint murals on the side of these huge toolboxes for the flight engineers. I did portraits of generals and of people who were retiring…I was also a calligrapher.

The generals would be like, "Come over here and do some artwork." It was awesome.

How long were you in the service?

P: Four-and-a-half years. I was honorably discharged. When I got out I was a sergeant. I got married and we had a baby, who is now thirty-four. Gas back then was a dollar a gallon and a pack of cigarettes was $1.87.

JS: Patrick and his first wife divorced in 1992 and he moved to California, where he worked in advertising.

P: I did commercials for Disney and Coors Light. It really was like "Mad Men." I do film editing now.

Have you always voted for Republican candidates?

P: I only voted for Ron Paul. I don't vote anymore.

JS: Dr. Ron Paul, like Keyes, was another politician whose be-liefs resonated with Patrick's. He first heard Paul speak in 2007, announcing his bid to be the 2008 Republican nominee for President. But when Paul didn't win the nomination, something Patrick still contests as manipulated, Patrick retreated from political life, including at the ballot box.

    When asked why he doesn't vote, Patrick said his reasons began several years before, after a growing cynicism after 9/11 with what he believes were unsavory connections between high-ranking government officials and one of the world's largest investment firms, The Carlyle Group.

P: I knew the government was involved with 9/11. It was as clear as the nose on your face. That really pissed me off. Frank Carlyle had been roommates with Donald Rumsfeld and I started really looking into it. (George H. W. Bush's youngest son) Marvin Bush was head of security for the World Trade Center complex. There was a specific addendum (on the insurance policy) that if the World Trade Center was hit by aircraft (there would be a larger payout)…but you'll never hear this stuff.

    This was part and parcel why I got so angry about our government.

JS: The final nail, per se, occurred in early 2008 during the Re-publican Presidential Debates.

P: I saw this little man, Dr. Ron Paul. He was making all this sense about the war (in Iraq and Afghanistan). He talked about how the United States was bombing others, and how he took his marching orders from the Constitution. It was nice to see someone Libertarian. I had never heard these views before. I thought, "Finally, an honest person."

What (Paul) said resonated with my heart and I knew it to be factually true. I got on his volunteer team; I did some ads and billboards for him. We raised money that was a lot for back then, but it wouldn't be now.

JS: Patrick went on to explain why he threw up his hands in defeat after the 2012 Presidential Election when he felt Paul was cheated from being the Republican nominee.

P: It was 2012 when we got ripped off. I was an alternate delegate and Ron Paul was winning all these states. The GOP shut down the delegates to Ron Paul because they knew he'd win and they wanted Mitt Romney. I was like, "Look at these liars!"

What do you think of Ron Paul's son, Rand Paul?

P: Love him. He's a little caustic at times, but I don't care about people's personalities—it's what they say. The truth is the truth no matter who says it. Is he perfect? Nobody's perfect.

So, no other candidates have gotten you excited since 2008?

P: No. Just Justin Amash; he's from Palestine. Don't get me started on Israel and Palestine.

JS: As of this writing, Justin Amash serves as the U.S. Representative for Michigan's third congressional district, holding this seat since 2011. Originally a member of the Republican Party, Amash became an Independent in July, 2019.

Where do you currently live and do you get involved in local politics there?

P: I live in Oklahoma and no, because local politics is a strange beast.

What is your ideal view for America? What issues are important to you?

P: Number one: We're taxed for everything. People are like, "This is for the road," but that's not taxing. That's a bond that should be voted on by the people locally. Taxes are taken out of your paycheck. We have the FICA, Social Security, all kinds of different taxes taken out. The gas station taxes…

We're told, "We're going to tax you to build that bridge," but then that tax never gets taken off.

We're taxed like crazy and yet the federal deficit is astronomical.

Then we have the Department of Education. People say we need to be educating people. I agree, but it should be small communities governing themselves and they can educate their children the way they see fit. It shouldn't be mandated or forced under threat of violence.

It's scary what's happening in this country. The federal government is infiltrating every smallest action of everyone. If you don't do something that the government asks you to do… they're not asking you, they're telling you. They will get their armed thugs in their cute little costumes with their fake badges and come with **your** guns to take you away under threat of violence.

(2020 Democratic Presidential hopeful) Beto O'Rourke admitted it when he said, "We will come and take your guns."

Well how are you going to do that? It's simple. They are going to use their guns to take your guns. That is what the

21

second amendment was written for; it's the perfect example of why we need any guns we like.

As soon as the government takes the people's guns... Every single communist country, as soon as you take people's guns away, the people get killed. That's why it's so scary now. People never look at those things in the proper perspective. I think my constitutionalist, libertarian view is grounded in common sense and logic.

Why not say you're a Republican? It sounds like your views align with the Republican Party.

P: Neo-cons, the new conservatives, are crazy. There's a group called the New American Century that wrote "Re-building America's Defenses," which calls for the invasion and regime change of seven countries in the next decade. On that board were Rumsfeld, the Bushes, and the Cheneys. I can't stand any of them.

What do you think of Donald Trump?

P: I think he's a trip. When he was campaigning in 2016 the news said he ripped off all the workers at his casino in Atlantic City and I'm like, "That isn't true." Trump is from where I'm from and I have a first-hand source that it isn't true. I went to high school with someone who worked at (Trump's) casino and did get paid. When Trump went public with his company, the first thing he did was reward his employees, which was amazing.

Does he say crazy and wild stuff? I've heard crazier and I've heard wilder.

When people say they can't stand Trump I say, "How was the Three Strikes Law? Trump repealed that."

"So you don't like CBD oil?"

"You didn't want that woman to be released from prison after twenty years?"

I got $2,000 in child tax credits this year instead of the $1,000 under Obama. Trump made all those things happen.

But you didn't vote for Trump?

P: No, and the reason why I don't vote for people...I could've bet $1,000 that Hillary was going to win. That's why Trump did win. They didn't think he would win. They knew Ron Paul was going to win; that's why they bashed him. If they knew then what they know now, they would have bashed Trump far more, or ignored him completely. That's what they did to Ron Paul. They ignored him.

If you thought Trump had a chance of winning in 2016, would you have voted for him?

P: I can't vote for someone who doesn't do anything about the real problems in the world. We shouldn't have three hundred military bases in more than one hundred countries around the world; it's ridiculous. There's a meme that says, "Iran placed a country right next to our military bases." I'm like, leave those people alone.

Why do you choose not to vaccinate your two young kids?

P: People say, "You're going to get our kids sick since you do not vaccinate," and I'm like, "Are you going to give your husband herpes?"

They say, "How can I if I don't have the disease?"

"Aha! Point proven. Back off lady!" I say.

Is it more that you don't want the government telling you what to do, or that you don't want to put vaccines in your kids' bodies?

P: A little of both. Obviously, I don't want the government to tell me what to do. They (the government) should be mere referees, especially in contractual law. But also, there is no way anyone's going to stick a dirty needle in my kid. Within five minutes after birth they give babies a Hepatitis B shot. Why would you inject a live, dead, or an attenuated virus into a child whose immune system is just beginning to form? Vaccinations have never saved one single life in all of history; it's sanitation that does. Refrigeration, toilet, sewer system, water treatment plants, healthy living, healthy eating, showering, wiping with toilet paper, getting rid of rats and their fleas, disposing of the dead…all little things.

You're very complex. Most people fall into one camp or another. I'm trying to categorize you, but you are outside the box.

JS: Patrick replied with a laugh.

P: Yeah, people that think for themselves are scary.

Is your choosing to homeschool in the same vein, then, as why you choose not to vaccinate? Why are you a homeschool pro-ponent?

P: The fairy tale myth that homeschooled kids aren't social isn't true. They are super social, but I don't want my kids to be picked on or bullied. I also don't want my kids to be taught by somebody who's getting their instructions from the federal government. That's what's wrong with the Board of Education.

Number one, they're moochers. They just take our money and there's so much money that goes to the bureaucracy that never even reaches the kids. Next, they're putting so much social engineering in public school kids to think a certain way and I don't want my kids to think that way.

I love the *Captain Fantastic* movie where Viggo Mortensen's character and his wife raise their six kids in the actual forest and teach them survival skills. I love when the father says to his daughter, "What do **you** think the Bill of Rights are?"

And she says, "The government shouldn't be interfering with your life, and these are protected rights born from our natural rights."

It's a beautiful movie.

JS: Patrick continued to tie his view on homeschooling back to his stance on vaccines.

P: It's all connected. I ask adults, "Are you up to date with your vaccinations? Are you up to date with all seventy-two of the CDC vaccination doses?"

And they're like, "I don't know… "

I then say, "Have you given all thirty-six CDC vaccination doses to your children by the time they're five?"

They say, "That's between me and my doctor!"

Bingo! Aha! It is between a patient and a doctor. Nobody else. Not the government or the state, but these kids… There's formaldehyde and all kinds of carcinogens injected into these vaccines. There is all kinds of crazy stuff that attacks the immune system "to get a better reaction," they say.

JS: Patrick went on to describe what he thinks is corruption in big pharmaceutical companies, specifically that they don't have the best interests of people as a top priority—they value profits instead.

P: The CDC owns patents to vaccinations. It's like the fox guarding the henhouse. They don't care about our children; they care about profits, period. It's nasty. Yet if you don't vaccinate, you're told you're a danger and a threat to your friends and your community and society at large.

People say, "How dare you?" to me.

I have also had thousands of mothers tell me they were pro-vaccine before their kids were injured, before vaccines attacked their kids' immune systems. In 1988 it was one in 50,000 children who developed autism. Now it's one in thirty. The autism spectrum disorder begins with an allergy to something, like peanuts. They put peanut oil in the vaccinations, you know.

That was the thought by some ten to fifteen years ago. Do you believe autism is linked back to vaccines?

P: No, autism is caused by vaccines. Now people bring up this fallacy—correlation is not equal to causation. For people who are pro-choice, I say my wife and I are pro-choice about vaccinations. The government shouldn't be involved.

I also think it's so horrible what we have done to our environment. The large polluters can buy carbon credits and continue to pollute. There's a massive amount of trash in our oceans.

What angers me the most about man made climate change is that all of our gases are CO_2 (carbon dioxide). Plastic is a scourge to the Earth and it should be eliminated. We didn't have it when we were kids. We had wax paper everything: straws, containers, Chinese take-out containers. Wax paper is paraffin and paper. It can be burned, thrown into a volcano, and it won't hurt the environment. Plastic is killing everything.

Another thing they're doing... eight hundred million trees died in California in the past five years. They don't know why, but they're spraying stuff in the sky. I recommend everyone read a book by Robert F. Kennedy, Jr. called "Crimes Against Nature." It is the saddest thing you'll ever read.

What is a trusted news source for you?

P: I get my news everywhere. I usually take what several different sources say, measure it, and put all the pieces together like a puzzle to make my own opinion. I put a piece of what Drudge says with a "Huffington Post" piece, for instance. YouTube is a medium not unlike the newspaper. I get news on Facebook...Bing... Duck Duck Go.

I listen for the way language is used. I could look at CNN and tell they're telling lies just by the way they say something.

Are you registered to vote?

P: No. One bad thing is I don't get called for jury duty. I used to love going to jury duty because I controlled the whole thing (laughs). I do miss that.

There's never that feeling that you can save anything if even by your one vote? I've never met someone more passionate about politics but who doesn't take part in the process.

P: Right. People say if you don't vote, you can't complain. I say it's the opposite: when you vote, you have nothing to complain about. So, I figure I have the right to complain.

Is this all a weight on you? Do you think the world is crazy?

P: I do say the world is crazy a lot. So I go back to my small community of like-minded people and govern myself. I won't force my views on you, and you don't force your views on me.

Steve

"A World View"

Born—1944 in Boston, Massachusetts
Political Identity—Liberal Republican

Steve has moved every few years for his entire life. As a child he and his two younger sisters, and their parents, moved across the country and back again, between Boston, California, Connecticut, New Orleans, and back to California all by the time Steve graduated from high school. "My dad was transferred every two to three years; it was part of my growing up," Steve explained. "It was difficult to make long-term friends."

As an adult he moved just as often between different countries, even different continents. There would be upsides, however. Steve described that the insights he had during his travels abroad are key to his political shaping.

While serving in the United States Army during the Vietnam War Steve lived in Germany, where he met his first wife. He then worked for the United States State Department from 1972 to 1994, a career that took him around the globe, offering him a macro view of America, giving him a broader perspective of its complexities than most people ever get to experience. While many believe Americans are too entrenched in partisanship and party loyalty, from his experience, Steve believes Americans are still much more likely to cross the political aisle than citizens living in other countries. While some Americans have a doom and gloom outlook on everything from race relations to our elections, Steve has come to the conclusion that in America all signs point to general civility and a healthy democracy.

Like Patrick, Steve was born into an Irish Catholic, east coast family, which both described as a sure way for one to identify as a Democrat. And though the culture of being an Irish Catholic Democrat was a legacy that ran deep in both men's families, particularly through the stories that were passed down to them, they both carved out different political identities, apart from the circumstances into which they were born, as adults. They did this by doing their own research and thereby coming to their own conclusions.

While Patrick unequivocally "hated the war" in Vietnam, Steve saw America's role as a needed course of action to safeguard America and the rest of the world from dictatorial regimes.

Steve comes across as quiet and humble, but he is resolute when discussing his beliefs. He has a fresh perspective on what he thinks causes anti-American sentiments abroad, something he witnessed in places that he has lived, including Ethiopia. Steve was also clear about what he thinks can be done about it. After experiencing what it is like to live in countries with different forms of government, Steve shared why he thinks America's system not only works but is superior. And while he may have shed his Democratic Party roots, his lifelong Catholic faith continues to be one of his greatest guides when he votes.

What is your earliest memory of being shaped politically?

S: As a child I picked up on that everyone was a Democrat and that that was an expectation.

My mom had come from a large Irish Catholic family and, politically, they were Democrats. I was closer to my mom's side of the family. In Boston at that time, and for years before that, Boston was a Democratic Party place. If you were Irish, you were definitely going to be a Democrat. It was party line voting and party line support. My (maternal) grandfather was a fireman in Boston. He was born in the United States, but all of his brothers were born in the old country.

My parents would tell stories of how Irish people had been heavily discriminated against in this country. For instance, they remembered seeing signs in stores that said, "Irish need not apply."

My parents also experienced discrimination to a degree. My dad's side was not Catholic, but he experienced discrimination for being from Canada. He used to tell me that when he was a kid he "caught hell for being a foreigner" because he had an accent.

You were raised with parents who were Democrats yet identify now as a Republican. When did this change?

S: I had a slow awareness of politics about the time I decided to major in political science in college. I didn't go into it because I was highly political or aware. I just figured I'm terrible at math, so engineering was out. Maybe because I had moved so much as a child, but I was interested in learning about new places and different, foreign lands.

I went to a junior college and you could have a student deferment from the (Vietnam) draft as long as you were making "normal" academic progress. It had taken me three years to complete my freshman and sophomore years, so I got a letter from the draft board saying that since I hadn't made normal progress, I was going to be drafted at the end of the semester.

I didn't want to be drafted because I'd go in as an infantryman. I wanted to have choice over what I did if I had to go, so I decided to enlist instead, but I wasn't sure what I wanted to do. But if you were drafted you only served for two years. If you enlisted, you had to enlist for three years. I guess that's the price of admission.

I dropped out of school and checked into what the opportunities were with each of the service branches. I came across counter-intelligence operations and thought that sounded interesting. I had read a book about these soldiers in World War II who were involved in Civil Affairs, which is through the Army. That's what I was looking for. So, I enlisted in the Army.

JS: It was in the mid-1960s and opposition to the Vietnam War was building when Steve made this decision.

S: It was probably when I was around twenty, about the time I went in the Army, I really started to change my thinking. I was a supporter of the Vietnam War. I thought it was the right thing to do because the country was in danger of communist takeover. To one degree or another I accepted the idea of the Domino Theory—that if one country fell, another would. As it turns out, that wasn't totally true. Thailand didn't fall, but Cambodia and Laos did.

JS: The reality of what was happening in Vietnam was still unknown to most Americans.

S: A friend of mine in Army Intelligence school had said, "I think I'm going to volunteer for Vietnam…if I volunteer for Vietnam, will you too and we'll go as buddies?"

JS: Steve agreed but the next day, on his way to ask the sergeant, his friend stopped him and said he had reconsidered for job security reasons, a twist of irony that would show itself to the rest of the world in short course.

Steve assumed he would go to Vietnam anyway, but he was stationed in Germany.

S: That's where I met my first wife. My only other exposure to another country was visiting Tijuana and Montreal as a kid.

JS: Steve remained in the Army for three years and then went back to college, graduating with a bachelor's and master's degree in political science and international relations. "The GI Bill is a very good thing," he said.

After working in the private sector for a few years, Steve went on to work for the United States State Department from 1972 to 1994.

How did you end up working for the State Department?

S: Although my private sector work was interesting and successful, I wanted a different and perhaps larger challenge, and I still had the urge to travel overseas. Vietnam was still going on, but the military was pulling out at that point. During my search I stumbled on the (State Department's) Office of Security. Given my military service and education it seemed like a good fit. But, the State Department didn't hire many people then. Normally a new agent was hired only if someone retired or died. It took a while, but an opening occurred. I was the last person they hired under that system.

I worked in the Office of Security, which is now called the

Diplomatic Security Service. It is one of the oldest law enforcement agencies in the United States. It goes back more than one hundred years. I was hired as a Special Agent/ Regional Security Officer (RSO). RSO's are special agents posted to U.S. diplomatic posts overseas. My anticipation was that I'd go to the Embassy in Saigon for my first assignment in about eighteen or twenty-four months, but after about a year I was suddenly told I was going to Brussels, Belgium. I was surprised. My daughter, who was just a little over a year old, my then wife, and I moved to Brussels.

What did your job entail?

S: In the United States it was investigations—background, criminal, passport, and visa fraud, as well as protection of dignitaries. There was a fair amount of passport fraud. Much of it involved drug smuggling and drug related activity. I was supposed to interview Timothy Leary, but was transferred just before.

JS: Leary was an American psychologist who famously advocated for the use of psychedelic drugs under controlled conditions for therapeutic benefits.

S: Leary's philosophy morphed into free drugs and free love for all. His followers engaged in significant illegal drug related activities which included passport fraud and drug smuggling and sales.

JS: Overseas Steve was a Regional Security Officer (RSO) in charge of security at United States Embassies and for the official Americans living there. During his tenure Steve lived in Brussels, Belgium; Addis Ababa, Ethiopia; Vienna, Austria; Ankara, Turkey; and eventually as a site manager for a project in New Delhi, India, and then back to Ethiopia.

He retired in 1994 and then worked in the security departments for a New York bank, high-tech Silicon Valley company, private security consulting company, a professional recruitment firm, and an international engineering and construction company before retiring completely several years ago.

What did you learn about the United States while living abroad?

JS: Steve went on to describe how seeing different forms of government, apart from what he was accustomed to in the U.S., was a startling comparison.

S: Much of Europe has a parliamentary form of government, which is quite different from ours. A lot of countries in Europe also have a monarchy, where the king or queen is the head of state but they're not the head of government.

In the United States we have the head of state and head of government in one person—the President. We elect our representatives differently than they do in a parliamentary system. We select individual candidates. In parliamentary systems voters often select lists of candidates and a "no confidence" vote can bring down the leadership or even the entire government. When we elect a president it's for four years. Our president can be removed through an involved impeachment process, which is relatively rare.

JS: This interview took place in August, 2019, several months before the process to impeach President Donald Trump began.

S: In the parliamentary system a complete term is not guaranteed. We recently saw that in the U.K. where there was a change in leadership. It's very different and the attitudes of the people are quite different; they are more closely associated with their parties than we are. They generally vote for a complete party ticket rather than, well, "I like this person and their ideas so I'm going to vote for them."

What did you think about those differences?

S: I could see the differences in action, and I frankly don't care for that system. I think our system provides us with more stability and is more representative of the interests of the people. It also provides a greater opportunity for real consensus and discussion of different ideas. Many other countries have strict party discipline and don't tolerate political beliefs or speech that doesn't agree with the party leadership.

Generally speaking, Americans have less party loyalty and vote across party lines more than their counterparts in parliamentary systems. And we have significant, scheduled elections, more often than most other countries—every two years for the House of Representatives. I believe all of that is a sign of a good, healthy democracy.

Did you find you grew to appreciate America while living overseas?

S: Yes. Seeing the differences in the way governments operate and seeing the effects of history on our society versus the effects of history on, for example, European societies…We come from a different place, a better place.

My ex brother-in-law (from Germany) was very politically aware. During the time I was in the Army and first went overseas with the Foreign Service, we were having a lot of racial problems in America. There was rioting in cities; we had had the assassinations of Martin Luther King Jr. and Bobby Kennedy. It was a pretty raucous time here in the United

States.

My ex brother-in-law liked to goad me and say they didn't have that going on in Europe. It was true at the time. European countries were pretty homogenous until the 1980s and '90s in terms of their racial and ethnic make-up. The United States has never been that homogenous, which is one of our strengths.

JS: Similar to saying that Americans are more likely to cross the political aisle than Europeans are, I was surprised when Steve said that America integrates immigrants more smoothly, an issue that has divided many Americans particularly in recent years.

S: Integrating foreigners into their societies has been a difficult thing for all European countries to grapple with. Compared to America, I think they have been unsuccessful; it's why they have trouble with homegrown terrorists. It's because they haven't been able to assimilate people into their society.

In Germany I had a friend who was a gypsy. His passport and ID card said "stateless," which meant he didn't have German citizenship or any other citizenship, even though he was born and raised in Germany.

We have our problems in the United States, but the way we've integrated people racially and culturally is spectacular by comparison.

Did you have any big takeaways about what you think works and what doesn't on a global scale?

S: I was transferred to Ethiopia after Brussels. It's difficult to sum up what it was like in Ethiopia. About two years before I got there, Emperor Haile Selassie had been deposed, imprisoned, and murdered, as were a large number of his family. When I got to Ethiopia it was a communist dictatorship, or as they might say, "a socialist people's government." But it doesn't work without massive control of the people through the police, military, and paramilitary organizations.

In Marxist philosophy there are councils - there are various levels and each level is elected by the immediate lower level until the person at the top is reached. It's a very regimented way of living. The country resembled Stalinist Russia or Maoist China—that is to say, you either supported the government, or went to jail, or worse.

In Addis Ababa, the capital of Ethiopia, I saw groups of young teenagers marching in the streets carrying broomsticks, or things that looked like rifles. They would be marching in support of the government. There were neighborhood committees with an area they were responsible for and they ran that area the way they saw fit, enforcing the rules with their own armed vigilantes. The vigilantes were armed with everything from hunting rifles, which the government had confiscated from private citizens, to RPG's (Rocket Propelled Grenades), so that they could be a formidable group, even though they were totally untrained.

Those in charge manipulated the population. There was always a food shortage or a social protest that was manipulated. There were anti-American demonstrations that were reported in the newspapers as spontaneous. The government organized these "spontaneous" demonstrations weeks in advance. The people were told to create a threatening disturbance, to, say, storm the American embassy at nine o'clock and chant a particular slogan. If they didn't show up, they were told that their rations of meat wouldn't be available. So people showed up, whether they believed in imperialism of the United States or not. Numbers of people would show up, but after roll call they would slip away. Many of the people in the street liked the U.S. but needed their food rations so they did what they were told.

39

To see these young people...these young teenagers, marching around the streets was, to me, repugnant. It was clear to me that the philosophy I saw in action promises much and delivers only hardship. It doesn't work anywhere.

That experience, and other less dramatic ones, good and bad, has helped reinforce a feeling of pride, patriotism, and gratitude for our country even with all its shortcomings. Our Constitution is not only our fundamental law but it's also the fundamental description of what we are striving to be. Few other countries are as committed to making life better for its citizens and the world than we are.

What do you think when you hear anti-American sentiments today? What do you think that is rooted in?

S: Much of the world has no real understanding of American society or our political process. Many have a gross misunderstanding of who we are. A lot of it comes from the inaccurate information they get from TV and now the Internet. For years overseas the most popular show on television was "Baywatch." What does that tell you about American society? It tells people we're shallow, spoiled, rich, materialistic, and don't much care about others in the wider world.

We should show what America is through cultural activities, cultural exchanges, and through American libraries. Most every embassy, particularly if it's a large one, has a separate American library. And they have cultural activities, films, books. It used to be called the U.S. Information Service. For the most part, it is an attempt for us as the United States government to show what America is in a more truthful and factual manner.

Do you think we're better off in America from a security standpoint, and/or from the way the rest of the world perceives

the United States, compared to twenty or thirty years ago?

S: I think much of the world still doesn't have an accurate enough knowledge base to figure us out.

Our culture is so dynamic due to technology and our natural desire to follow change that others, even some of our closest allies, find it difficult to understand us. We are a generous and altruistic society. Unfortunately, that message and behavior is often overlooked. Much of that altruism comes from our everyday citizens. It can be seen in international volunteerism, for example in our disaster response teams that respond to disasters all over the world. Many of those people are not paid. We're not shallow and selfish. And we should make sure our friends and non-friends have a better understanding of who we really are. That will improve the way we are perceived and also increase our national security.

This country isn't crashing and burning like some think it is. And I don't think that giving the federal government a larger role to play will improve the situation.

JS: Steve said that his belief that a limited federal government works best is one of the main reasons he identifies with the Republican Party.

S: In my observation the more the government is involved, the less responsive it is to the needs of the people. In a really small country that might be okay, but the United States is a big country both in terms of geography and population. The federal government is not in the position to take care of the day to day needs of the people. The larger the federal government grows, the more bureaucratic and less responsive it becomes.

State and local governments understand the needs of the people in a way far better than the people in Washington can. Our national government needs to focus on national and

41

international level issues: the economy, environment, and appropriate associated regulation; national defense policy and implementation; international relations; and areas that states are unable to adequately address. We have thousands of career government employees who would rather be doing that than developing difficult or unworkable regulatory solutions to issues the states should handle.

We need ongoing programs to keep our armed forces properly sized, well trained, and equipped with the most advanced equipment. Participation in international organizations is a requirement and a strong foreign affairs structure is imperative. Diplomacy is our first line of defense. It's been said that the Defense Department has more musicians than the State Department has Foreign Service Officers—there needs to be some balance there. We need more diplomats in more places explaining and justifying our positions, negotiating agreements, and offering help and assistance in places that need it, which goes back to altruism. Prevention is always better than remedy.

The world recognizes what we are. In order to expand our positive influence and make us more secure we need the world to know *who* we are.

In business you have to pay attention all of the time to your base of customers. When your needs change, you have to change with them, or you go out of business. The government doesn't have that same motivation to some degree to maintain itself. A number of years ago people were looking at the way the government was buying things. There was a famous story about the Defense Department buying food to serve in military mess halls. The food intake description was sixty-five pages long. That is just one example of the tremendous regulations we have.

Have you always voted for Republicans?

S: No. I've voted across party lines. How closely a candidate's speech, and past behavior parallels my beliefs, is more important to me than a party label.

Why do you identify as a *liberal* Republican?

JS: Point by point, Steve rattled off positions that he equates with "liberal Republican."

S: The Catholic Church talks about social justice. I like that term. There are people out there who need the help of the government and justice demands that we support them. I donate to, and support, church based social programs that assist the unemployed and provide social services to the needy. I vote in favor of such public programs.

I believe in strong foreign aid programs—even for countries that don't always support our foreign policies.

I'm strongly pro-life. I believe that abortion stops a beating heart and that abortion on demand is not a right, period.

On big holidays I fly a really large American flag which flew over the American Embassy in Ankara, Turkey. The flag was a gift given to me when I left.

The government needs to use its massive purchasing power to reduce the cost of prescription drugs.

In years past the federal government has provided grants of money, with few strings attached, to states to help support their various social welfare programs. This was done without expanding federal bureaucracy, which would drive up costs and diminish the impact of those programs. Continuing and expanding the use of faith-based programs is a particularly fruitful way of reaching the needy. Costs are low, volunteerism is high, and money and services get to where they are most effective.

I think of the Republican Party as the "big tent" party and

the Democratic Party as less inclusive, but requiring more and more absolute support of the party platform by way of litmus tests, less open discussion, and no opposing opinions. There are bound to be plenty of people I don't agree with and that's fine.

In the end, I don't have a corner on truth. I believe we can all learn from one another and, even if we can't get our way, we should be willing to negotiate and compromise.

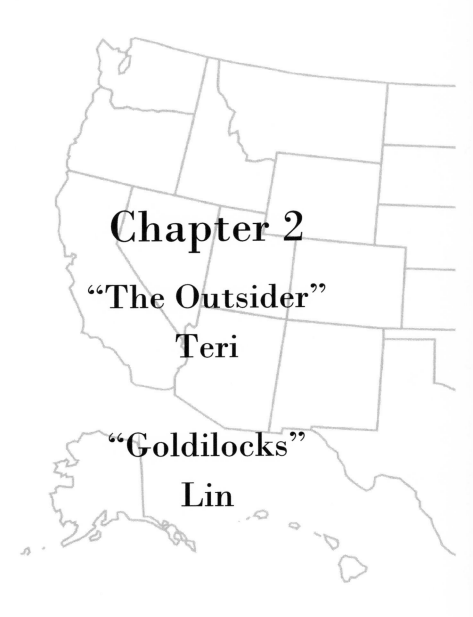

Chapter 2

"The Outsider"
Teri

"Goldilocks"
Lin

Teri
"The Outsider"

Born—1970 in Taiwan
Political Identity—Independent, Leans
Progressive Democrat

In 1975 five-year-old Teri emigrated with her parents to the United States from Taiwan. Unlike many people who come to the United States for greater opportunities, Teri explained that wasn't the case for her family, who came under threat of persecution. While physically safe once the family settled in the San Francisco Bay Area city of Fremont, it wasn't a panacea to Teri; feelings of discrimination and a perpetual feeling that she didn't fit in, with neither her white nor Asian classmates, continued and remained a large component of her political shaping. Teri felt like a stranger in a strange land, poignantly symbolized by the bicentennial Fourth of July celebrations that kicked off just as her family arrived in America.

For company, Teri threw herself into reading books and watching the news, which made her not only passionate about politics years before she could legally vote, but also more politically astute than arguably any fifth grader in America. President Ronald Reagan and his administration played a pivotal role in Teri's shaping. It was the first election in which she wished she could vote, and she still remembers how she felt when her mother informed her she would be voting for Reagan. His years in office, which occurred during Teri's teen years, led her to a lifelong mistrust of Republican lawmakers as touting values that were contrary to her own, particularly pertaining to national defense and immigration. Teri, so afraid of war, explained how she lived rebelliously out of fear she didn't have long to live.

Teri's mother needed a blood transfusion after she had an ectopic pregnancy in 1985, at which time she contracted the HIV virus. To this day, Teri blames the Reagan administration for "dragging its feet" on AIDS research, and that being proactive could have prolonged her mother's life.

Brutally honest, Teri isn't shy to share her thoughts on other issues that make her blood boil, from greed and corruption being at the roots of all evil, to one of the greatest gifts she ever received: being raised by a stay-at-home father at a time when that was rare.

Why did your parents move to the United States?

T: My father was blackballed by the university where he taught for being a western philosophy scholar. Before Nixon opened up China, and Taiwan lost its seat on the security council, Taiwan was considered to be the Chinese government by westerners. When Nixon went over there, they gave the seat to the communists. I don't argue with the decision to do that as much as the consequences, which destroyed my father's career. There was a huge backlash in Taiwan against western thought because they screwed the Taiwanese.

My father taught at NTU (National Taiwan University), which is the premiere university in Taiwan, and they didn't want the "best and brightest" being infected by western thought. My father was told he needed to change his focus and teach something else, become something else, or quit. Luckily, he had enough connections that he became a journalist, but he wasn't happy. He was born to be a professor. He thinks at a deeper level than just about anyone. My father is the most brilliant person I know.

Was there any upside to moving to the United States?

T: Unlike most Asian immigrants, we didn't come here to make money. Unless they come as refugees, if you talk to many Asian immigrants, they think of America as a shiny path to gold. They come here for the opportunities.

In my father's circumstance there wasn't a good, practical reason to leave Taiwan. My father was fairly privileged there. He had a master's degree at a time when most people didn't have bachelor's degrees. But we left for ideological and intellectual reasons. That's one of the reasons we're different from so many Asian immigrants. It's why I've always been frustrated by the superficial, materialistic attitudes of so many people in the Bay Area. It's aggravating that it's all about money, money, money.

What is your earliest memory of living in the United States?

T: I remember 1976, when the United States celebrated its Bicentennial. I spoke very little English, but I remember it was overwhelming. It was such an insanely, superficially patriotic environment. People were going crazy about being American in this knee-jerk, jingoistic, "We're number one" kind of way.

I couldn't relate because In Taiwan we were not that proud of being Taiwanese. We were under martial law. The whole point of being Taiwanese was to reinvade China and take it back.

As a little kid I figured that's the way America was—super patriotic all the time. It was overwhelming, but I tried not to think too hard on it.

Did you have any trouble assimilating since you were so young?

T: I blundered along and did my best to assimilate. I felt "lesser than" for being different. People in Fremont tried to condition me to shed my differences. I got so much praise from teachers for learning English so fast and without an accent. People would say, "On the phone you sound just like an American," or, "I didn't realize you aren't white… You're just like everyone else if no one sees you."

That's been an undercurrent. For a lot of years I felt like there was something wrong with me that I couldn't fix. It was like my Asian-ness was a disability. It was a really traumatic upbringing.

Isn't there a significant Asian population in the Bay Area, in particular Fremont?

T: I didn't live in the Asian part of Fremont. We were the poor Asians. The wealthy Asians were in Mission San Jose (another neighborhood within Fremont). I knew most of those Asian kids; their fathers were in tech. Many of them worked at IBM. Most of their moms didn't work. There were a lot of stay-at-home Asian moms back then.

My mom was a nurse and my dad was a stay-at-home parent for most of my childhood. He couldn't get a job because no one was going to hire someone with a philosophy degree from Taiwan. Do you know how many men would be emasculated by that? The trope was that many men in that situation would beat their wives and become alcoholic, but my father was a really good parent. He would pick me up from school and take me to the park or to the library; he researched free museums. Even though we were broke, he did his best to expose me to as much culture as possible.

I'm grateful my father was the one who had the time to raise me. I feel bad for my mother, though, that from the moment she arrived in this country she had to work her butt off to support a family. She was all of twenty-eight years old. Neither of my parents had it easy.

Did things get easier or harder as you got older?

T: We moved to San Francisco when I was ten. It was like another world. Suddenly being Asian was not a big deal. I started fifth grade there and I think twenty-four or twenty-five of the thirty students were Asian. I lived near Chinatown and suddenly I was another face in the crowd. It was both wonderful and negating. '

When did you become interested in politics?

T: The 1980 election was my first awareness. It was the three-way election (between Ronald Reagan, Jimmy Carter, and John Anderson.)

John Anderson challenged Carter in the Democratic primary and didn't get it, but it was very close. So Anderson decided to run as an independent third party. Obviously that screwed Carter. It was a landslide (for Reagan) but I don't know if Anderson would have made a difference.

My fourth-grade teacher mentioned in passing that she was going to vote for Anderson and so I went home and I asked my mom who she was planning to vote for because she had just gotten her citizenship and was eligible to vote for the first time. My father had come from Taiwan just long enough after us that he wasn't qualified to vote in that election.

My mom told me she was going to vote for Reagan. I remember feeling disappointed, although I had no real understanding of why at the time. I just knew that I didn't like Reagan.

Why was that?

T: I did hear some of the pundits talk about how ridiculous it was that this former actor wanted to be president. That did form some of my thoughts about Ronald Reagan from the beginning. I didn't know anything about the right-wing hawkishness, just that basically he was unqualified and when he was Governor of California he did some things that were not good for California.

By then my mom had transitioned to be a lot like the other Asians. She cared about money and was more materialistic. She was very frustrated with my dad for not being able to earn a living and she really wanted to be a stay-at-home mom, although in retrospect I think she would have been terrible at it. Seeing my mother vote for Ronald Reagan and then seeing the disastrous eight years of the Reagan administration really had an impact on me.

What did you find disastrous about it?

T: The constant wars that were total bull. The rise in jingo-istic, quasi-fascist rhetoric. The way Republicans talked about immigrants. I knew they were mostly talking about Mexican Americans back then. I didn't feel personally attacked, but I knew, even as a kid, that if things got bad, if we didn't push back on that kind of rhetoric, they were going to come for us (foreign-born citizens). None of us were safe.

I knew that once that kind of nastiness takes hold of a society... I think I had already been reading things like Anne Frank by then. She was very, very popular in the late 1970s.

Most ten-year-old kids aren't as aware as you were. Why is that?

T: I was a very lonely child. I was an only child and I didn't have a lot of friends. I didn't have much to do other than read and watch TV. This was years before we had a billion channels. I would choose news or an educational program over sports. I was never that into sports until the 1986 World Series sucked me into baseball.

I also didn't have the same understanding as a lot of other kids because my parents weren't "real Americans." They weren't voting. We didn't talk about this stuff at the dinner table. Up until I was eight or nine years old the only thing political my parents talked about was what was going on in Taiwan. Taiwan was under martial law well into the 1980s. There was concern about the family; the last members immigrated to the United States in about 1979 and I think after that my family wasn't as worried because we were all out. Their political attention shifted to America about the same time.

And so my mom voted for Reagan. I felt a sense of betrayal, but I don't think she knew what she was doing because she wasn't paying attention.

Why do you think she voted for him?

T: I think she was influenced by her co-workers and you've got to remember, people hated Carter. The Iran Hostage Crisis (which lasted between 1979 and 1981) was a year and a half of American life when attention was on those poor people.

JS: Teri said that when she watched the 2012 film "Argo" starring Ben Affleck, it brought back painful memories of that time.

T: It reminded me how traumatized I was. I understood we were refugees. We had to escape the communists and go to a different place. Imagine all of the people in the U.S. taking off for Hawaii because the mainland was taken over by communists. That's how I felt.

I probably wouldn't be so unapologetically left-wing progressive if I didn't grow up under Reagan. I didn't feel safe for my entire childhood and adolescence. I was convinced I wasn't going to grow up to adulthood—that we were going to have nuclear annihilation. I lived my life as if I was going to die. This is one of the reasons I had such an angsty, rebellious adolescence, why I didn't care about my grades. I didn't plan to go to college. Nothing mattered because I was convinced Reagan was going to get us into a war with Russia and we were all going to die. That was basically how I felt until the Soviet

Union fell and the Berlin Wall collapsed. It was then that I thought, "Guess I do have to plan my life."

JS: It was also about this time that Teri's mother contracted the HIV virus after a blood transfusion. When Teri was fifteen her mother gave birth to another daughter. It wasn't until 1990, when Teri's mother was undergoing a life insurance physical, that she was told she tested positive for HIV. She died five years later when Teri's younger sister was ten years old.

I'm sure this experience also shaped your political beliefs, correct?

T: Oh yeah, the AIDS policy under Reagan. It was 1990 by the time my mom was diagnosed but of course she contracted HIV during the Reagan administration partly because the administration dragged its feet on funding test research. My mom died within a year of the, not cure, exactly, but a drug cocktail that would become a lifesaver, where AIDS wasn't a death sentence any longer but could be managed as a chronic disease. Right around the time my mom died in '95 that research broke through.

JS: It was 1985 that the first blood-screening test to detect HIV was licensed and then implemented by blood banks to protect the blood supply. Before this time, many hemophiliacs and other people who needed blood transfusions were unknowingly given infected blood.

T: Had the Reagan administration been faster on picking up the torch for research, they could have started testing the blood before she was infected. They started testing the blood within months of her getting her transfusion. We're very lucky that my sister dodged that bullet. She could have been born HIV positive. It doesn't pass the barrier into the uterus, but if my mom had chosen to breastfeed, my sister would have been infected. My mom didn't breastfeed for other reasons.

Have you always voted Democratic?

T: I registered Independent when I was eighteen and I haven't changed except when I wanted to vote in a Democratic primary. Now that we have open primaries I don't even do that anymore.

I've never been wholly invested in the whole party thing. I lean Democrat for sure. I've voted for Democrats in every major election, unless I throw my vote to a third party just to fight them, but it's more because I can't vote for a Republican than I'm so enamored with a Democrat.

Did your dislike for Reagan include his Vice-President, George H. W. Bush? You were probably not happy then when Bush senior was elected president?

T: God no. That was my first election I could vote. I voted for Dukakis. It didn't feel good; I saw the polls and heard people talking. I remember being so angry that my vote was going to be wasted.

I wanted the United States to be led by someone with a heart - someone who would see me and my people as genuine Americans who deserve to be here. There's always been this undercurrent of, "We let you be here, but if anything goes wrong, you'll be the first to go." It's like we're second class citizens or expendables. We'll get thrown under the bus if things go down.

Do you think you feel this way more because you are Asian or because you are from another country? Would you feel differ-

ently if you had blonde hair and blue eyes and were from Sweden?

T: It has a lot to do with looking visibly different. If I was a European immigrant I would probably have totally assimilated and thought, "I can't go back."

I sympathize with white Americans who have shed all of their ethnic identity markers over generations in order to assimilate and fit in, and now they're like, "Wait a minute, I could have remained Polish or Scandinavian? I could have had that connection to my heritage if only my parents and grandparents hadn't been pressured to deny it all to fit in."

I sympathize with that, but please don't take it out on us. We weren't the ones who forced you to reject your European heritage. You can't resent later ethnic immigrants for clinging to something that's important because we weren't allowed to disappear into American culture. I don't understand this misplaced anger. Be mad at the white Anglo-Saxons who wanted you to join them.

Asians are conditioned to feel like we don't deserve to be part of the American mainstream. We've internalized our foreignness, as though it's our fault. I want to push back hard on that.

How does that frame of thinking make you identify more with the Democratic Party?

T: It's really obvious which party really allows people of color a voice. They don't just trot out token people, or whoever they manage to find. There are actually high-powered people of color in the Democratic Party.

Even when Republicans think they're being nice, there is this condescending rhetoric. Even well-meaning attempts to be inclusive are cringe-inducing.

JS: Teri recalled how she felt when First Lady Barbara Bush described her grandchildren born to her son, Jeb, and his wife, Columba, a Mexican native.

T: Remember when Barbara Bush called her grandchildren the "brown ones"? There was this nudge-nudge, wink- wink, that they were a little different.

It's not that I don't have friends who are Republican. I'm going to be totally honest here—in terms of deep, analytical, and critical understanding of the world, in my opinion they don't have it. They like to keep things simple, prioritize their own comfort over larger, philosophical social questions, and it's getting hard to take.

Has there been a candidate anywhere—local, state, or nationally—who you see as having most of the qualities you think would be good for America?

T: I really like Alan Grayson.

JS: Grayson is an American politician who was the United States Representative for Florida's ninth congressional district and a member of the Democratic Party. He previously served as Representative for Florida's eighth congressional district from 2009 to 2011.

T: The fact that he struggled to win an election in Florida shows what's wrong with this country. He says what is on his mind; he's painfully blunt; he's honest, but he's right. Because I don't live in Florida, I can't vote for him.

Were you happy with President Obama?

T: I liked him a lot. He's smart, charismatic, and his heart was in the right place, but I think he was in over his head. He wound up getting pushed and pulled in directions he probably thought were abhorrent.

I don't think he really recognized how much of a figurehead the American President is. The president leads by speaking, through example; he can make nudges, but he's not a law maker. A lot of a president's legacy is rather amorphous— it's really what he can convince others to do while he's president, and not what he can do himself.

Every time a Democrat is elected they kick the can down the road because they're too chicken to confront the Republicans. Even Obama cared too much about reaching across the aisle instead of saying, "We're going to do this because it's the right thing to do."

If you can't get horrible people to work with you, the answer is not to water down your side.

How do you think the United States has changed since 1976?

T: I think we've gone bipolar. The blue cities are leading to hopefully a progressive future and then we have the red party, the rural, small town environments. All of the kids who grow up in those places and find it stifling come flocking to the blue cities.

The right leaning politics get more concentrated in those areas because the right-wing rhetoric and atmosphere are more oppressive, and so if you're a left-leaning minority in that environment, you just want to get out of there. Unless you have just the right personality that you can cheerfully argue with your friends and neighbors all the time, you're not going to want to stay. You're going to want to retreat to a blue city where you don't feel attacked all the time.

Conservative parents have been pushing their children away from home for generations. Then they don't understand why their children don't want to come home for Thanksgiving or understand why there's tension. It's because the parents are prejudiced and they make their children uncomfortable. Even in America, the youth still respect their elders. No one wants to go home at Christmas and fight with their parents or with their racist uncle. You want to be happy and celebrate with your family. I don't know how we're going to fix that.

Do you feel safe, or at least at home, living in San Francisco?

T: I am grateful to live in San Francisco, where I do feel safe, but it does become a trap. I can't go to eighty percent of the places in this country without feeling unsafe, and it's not just as a person of color but because there are guns everywhere.

JS: Teri has been a public high school teacher for more than twenty years. The 1999 Columbine High school shooting in Littleton, Colorado occurred when she was just beginning her career.

As a public school teacher what, if anything, do you think can be done to stop school shootings?

T: I've always said the best way to prevent a school shooting is to talk to the kids. If every kid had at least one adult on campus they felt safe sharing their problems with, we wouldn't have to worry about school shootings. This comes from disaffected, disengaged, isolated people who don't feel connected to anything. I'd be very curious if somebody would go to these surviving school shooters and ask, "Who was your favorite teacher on campus? Did you have one?"

I would venture to bet none of them would have. If that one adult would have existed, I don't think those students would have shot up the damn school.

That's one of the reasons why I always make it a priority to try to connect with my students as much as possible. I also just think it's good for them as writers to have somebody they can bounce ideas off of without thinking like they have to hold back. I think that's one of the most important things English teachers should do.

Do you want to say anything about current issues that continue to divide Americans, like what would be the best immigration policy?

T: I'm terrified. I really need to get my Taiwan passport in order in case I need to flee. They are talking about revoking American passports for naturalized citizens. If they do that, I will not have a passport and I will not be able to leave.

JS: Teri likened this fear to a theme shown in the 1966 musical "Cabaret." Set in Berlin in 1931, the story is at times light-hearted but is sobering as it shows the foreshadowing in the rise of the Nazi party.

T: We just went to see "Cabaret." The Jewish character is German-born and raised. He keeps saying, "I know my country. This too shall pass."

He gets sent to the gas chamber because he couldn't believe that his fellow Germans would treat him that way. I know perfectly well what my fellow Americans are capable of and I know that I am not going to be spared if it comes to that.

Trauma makes you always on alert for what the next source of danger is going to be.

Teri and Her Parents

Lin

"Goldilocks"

Born—1968 in Taiwan
Political Identity—Centrist, but Leans
Democrat

Like Teri (The Outsider), Lin spent her first five years in Taiwan, but instead of moving to the United States as Teri did, Lin and her family went to Canada, where she lived until she was thirty years old.

By 1999 Lin and her husband, tired of seeing much of their paychecks go toward taxes, emigrated to the United States with their young child. They would have two more children in the United States and during our interview Lin shared stark differences between the experiences of giving birth in Canada versus in the U.S.

Soon after the family made their new home in Texas, they were met by the razor-close election in 2000 between Al Gore and George W. Bush. In our interview Lin described her realization that every vote counts, (Bush didn't win the popular vote, but he won the Electoral College when he clinched Florida by a mere 500 votes) propelling Lin to seek U.S. citizenship so that she could make her voice heard at the ballot box.

Lin's shaping began once her parents, fearful of the strongholds of a communist regime, fled Taiwan only to move to a place where culture clashes continued to be a part of her reality in 1970s separatist Quebec. Like Teri, for much of her life Lin has felt like an outcast, even in her own communities. While Lin's two siblings now live in America as well, their parents remain in Canada because of the years they have paid into the tax system, hoping to reap rewards in their retirement.

It is no wonder that Lin identifies politically as a centrist; her multi-faceted experiences are difficult to categorize. During our conversation Lin spoke passionately about Taiwanese and Canadian history and the dichotomy she sees between Canada and the United States, particularly what she views as pros and cons between government run social programs versus free market capitalism, as seen between the two countries' differing healthcare systems. While both represent "too much" and "too little" to Lin, and she continues to seek policies with just the right balance, the metaphor of Goldilocks came to mind to describe her politics.

What do you think first shaped you politically?

L: I spent twenty-five years, my formative years, in Canada. We lived in Quebec, which is its own story. Canadians tend to vote not for what they want, but for what they don't want. It's always been like that. In Canada there is a three-party system. When I was growing up the Conservatives were very conservative, the Liberal Party was more central left, and the NDP (New Democratic Party) was more left-leaning than liberal. My parents always voted liberal. When I grew up, I tended to vote liberal too.

I grew up in a Jewish community in separatist Quebec, so you could not escape politics where I came from. That's where they had the bombings in the 1970s. It was the French Canadians versus anyone who wasn't French. After the French Canadians had been suppressed by the English when the British took over, laws had been created to protect the French culture. King Louis at the time said, "Okay, you have to give my people preferred status in the Constitution."

Because of this the French were classified as a lower class, but they got to keep their own French speaking schools and stay Catholic. Post-World War II the Catholic Church knew they needed more power, so they told people to have a lot of kids. Most French-Canadian families had ten, fifteen, twenty kids, but they were dirt poor. That huge generation of people who are baby boomers are a huge tax on Canadian society now.

These kids started to grow up in the 1960s. The French started coming into power in the 1970s. They banded together and started revolting because they had the numbers.

Inter-marrying between the French, Irish, and English is how people started to learn English and were able to go to school. As it's true now, you had to learn English in order to move on and have a better life.

My family got to Canada when the first Trudeau (Pierre)

was in power. Trudeau was half English and half French, which was very popular. He had tons of popularity and was famous around the world. Everyone was in love with him. He was very into social policies and he started all kinds of social programs. Trudeau really helped Quebec.

When 9/11 happened in the United States and security was beefed up, I was already used to that kind of security. Because of the separatists in Quebec and the violence, we had curfews in the 1970s. There were bombings at train stations and kidnappings of MP's (members of Parliament).

How was your family impacted by the culture clashes in Quebec?

L: We were caught because we had escaped Taiwan. We actually say "escape" because my dad always had the fear that the communists would come and take us if we didn't go first.

My dad was afraid of war and was afraid my brother would have been conscripted in the army, which he would have, if we'd stayed in Taiwan.

That's most of the reason why people left Taiwan in the 1970s - to escape Communist China. My parents had both escaped China as children. My dad was strongly anti-communist because the communists killed his dad and brother.

How were his father and brother killed?

L: Because my father joined China's Republic Army when he was thirteen. My father really had no idea what he was doing at the time. One of his buddies said to him, "Hey, the Revolution is going on. They need young men to join the Army!"

My dad thought it was a day camp.

JS: Lin laughed at this point, showing the incredulity she felt about her father's situation at the time.

L: So, he and his friend joined and they were shipped off to Taiwan. My father never saw his family again.

There was an iron curtain between China and Taiwan. It wasn't until my dad got to Canada that he could send letters back to his old hometown. He finally found a distant cousin who said, "Your father and brother were murdered by the communists when they found out you joined the Republic Army."

Most of us who have parents who came from Taiwan are coming from parents who are scared. This is why they left for either the United States or Canada.

My dad wanted to go to Canada, but when we got there we realized, "Wow, this is one of the most racist places in the world," because we didn't speak French.

It's still the rule of law today that children in Quebec have to go to French schools. If you're a new immigrant and you go through Quebec, which has the most lax laws because they're actually running out of people now, your children must go to French schools.

We got there in 1973 and the new law about having to go to French schools started in 1974. That's how I was able to go to English schools. My parents knew learning English was the ticket because you're surrounded by English, the United States is English, and the rest of the (Canadian) provinces are English. If you don't speak English you're not going to survive, which is still true today.

So I had the golden ticket. I actually had to show a ticket to go to English schools and I could pass that down to my children so that they could go to English schools. My younger sister, who was born in 1974, got in through this too. The ticket is good for the entire family.

How many languages did you speak as a child?

L: Three. At home I spoke Mandarin. At school I had English but because I was in Quebec I had to know French too. Since kindergarten to the end of high school I took mandatory French. All kids are pretty fluent in French there, but the cities are divided. One block can make a huge difference. The more French side is poorer.

Was your family religious?

L: No.

Fleeing communism, why did your family identify with the Liberal Party, do you think?

L: I think it was because we were immigrants and a visible minority. It has always seemed to me that the people who are more accepting of anyone different tend to be liberal, and the same has been in the United States. I have obviously been more accepted here by people who are left leaning.

Why did your parents choose to go to Canada?

L: It was way easier to emigrate to Canada than it was the U.S. In Canada every province runs its own immigration system, but once you get in, then you're under Canada as a whole. Quebec was the easiest to emigrate to because a lot of people didn't want to go there because of political turmoil.

Was it your family's dream to come to the United States?

L: No, well, from the outside we always watched American news; there was no escaping it. My father was always arguing, a political junkie, but it turned me off as a child. I didn't like to argue with him, but most of what he says makes sense. We only had two English channels. All the rest were French.

By the mid-1990s we had lived through two referenda— Quebec kept trying to separate from Canada and it got very emotional. It was basically east versus west. I was anglophone because I lived on the west side, the English side. I spoke French as a necessity to do business, whatever.

How did your parents meet?

L: In Taiwan. My mother's family were business people. They knew the communists were coming. At the time my mom only had a younger sister. They hopped on a ship and escaped when the Revolution was happening in China. Everyone was escaping to Taiwan or Hong Kong, which was British. They were getting out of there.

What year were your parents born?

L: My dad was born in 1932, and my mom in 1945.

That's a big age difference.

L: My mom left when she was five years old. My dad was thirteen. Any Chinese from Taiwan had an escape route. I even have a friend who came through Argentina.

What brought you to the U.S. when you were thirty years old and how did you choose which state to live?

L: Money, money, money (laughs). We were always looking to move to the U.S. and my husband was given an opportunity through his work. I was an architect for the federal government in Canada and my husband is an engineer. I wouldn't say we were high earners, but we were good earners. We got sick and tired of seeing so much of our paycheck go to the government. Because we are healthy and we're considered upper middle income we paid more, and we paid a lot more.

So your husband is Canadian as well?

L: He has a similar background. He's Chinese from Vietnam. He escaped the Vietnam War.

Did you apply for citizenship or a work visa? How did you come over?

L: The easiest, most economical way at the time was to have a company sponsor you. My husband's company was head-quartered in Dallas. There were openings and he knew the manager. His company was booming at that time. We could have gone to Boston or the Washington DC area, but we were coming over with Canadian dollars. The cost of living was much less in Texas.

The company paid for all of the moving expenses and they also got all of our immigration papers organized.

JS: Soon after arriving, Lin said she watched what she called the "election fiasco" of 2000 unfold, but she wasn't able to vote until 2008.

By 2008 did you have dual citizenship?

L: Yes. Canada lets you have as many citizenships as you want. The United States allows you to have one other, but if you travel abroad you must travel with your U.S. passport. If you choose to travel with your other passport, and let's say there's a war going on, or for some reason you get stuck overseas, they're not going to go save you.

I'm sure it's complicated, but if you had to explain to high school students what stands out as some of the biggest differences between living in the United States and Canada?

L: The big difference is money, money, money. Canadians are used to having social programs that they're willing to pay heavy taxes for. But if you make over $40,000, you're paying at least half of that in taxes. It was nice to know that if I lost my job in Canada I would still be okay. But I was healthy and hard-working. It broke my heart when I got my paycheck and saw how little I got to keep.

In the United States it's normal for professional families to live on one income while the other parent stays home to watch the kids. That's not true in Canada. It's the norm for both parents to work to get by. In the 1970s and '80s all of my friends' parents worked. I only knew one family where the mom got to stay home. They had five kids and the dad was a very successful jeweler.

So when I hear people say, "I'm going to move to Canada," I say, "Be careful what you wish for."

Since the government taxes everything in Canada, a gallon of gas costs five bucks even on a good day.

Also, when you live in a cold country like Canada, costs are going to be higher. A car, for instance, only lasts about five years because cars take such a beating. If you're the best driver on the road it doesn't matter, because there is no fault insurance in Canada; everyone pays. That's called socialism. If your neighbor is a bad driver, you're still going to pay as much as she does. A lot of people don't realize that. If you're a really good driver, you might get a discount after twenty years.

It's the same with healthcare. In the United States if you

don't take care of yourself, you're going to pay high medical expenses. In Canada everybody shares, everybody shares.

You have a perspective so many of us don't have. Based on all you're saying, like seeing socialist policies at work, why aren't you more on the right politically? Why do you consider yourself a left-leaning centrist and not more to the right?

L: I'm definitely for fiscal responsibility, so that's what I didn't like about Canada. I was trying to save money. It's not that I mind helping, not at all, but I worked so hard, and then I still ended up cutting one arm to go help somebody.

There were times when it was me who needed the help. When I had my first baby up there, that was another fiasco and another reason why I don't want social medicine. I nearly died because of mistakes they made up there. But then when I was home, they had tons of social programs. I did get depressed—I think every mom would get depressed if you have a baby in the middle of winter and it's dark fifteen hours a day. My husband traveled a lot for work. I was home with this crying baby. They sent social workers to check up on me. I didn't ask for it, they just did.

Did you like that?

L: At first I was a little offended. They sent me a Chinese lady. I was like, "What?!" But she would come over and hold the baby so I could take a nap and it was so nice.

How did they know to do that, to send someone to check in on you?

L: I was told that it's a social program that all the new moms get. I didn't even know I needed it, but it was so great. Another thing they had at the local hospitals was a breastfeeding clinic every day of the week. You could take your baby and weigh them, weigh their poopy diapers. You could even go to just vent. It was a little community that was a lifesaver to me.

In the U.S. they support breastfeeding but you have to pay for it, whereas if they say they support something in Canada, they put money behind it.

How many children did you have in Canada?

L: One. I had two more children in the United States and the experiences were so different. In Canada I asked the pediatrician if I could give a bottle only at night and was yelled at. When I came down here my new pediatrician said, "Sure."

Oh my gosh! I was even given samples of formula here in the U.S. I thought, "Oh my gosh! The U.S. is a capitalist society!" It was awesome. In Canada doctors' offices and hospitals are not allowed to give samples because it's seen as bribery among pharmaceutical companies.

It sounds like you didn't like the high taxes, but you appreciated the social programs in Canada.

L: Yes, but I didn't get to experience any benefits until I had a baby. As a single, healthy person I never saw any of it. It was a huge burden off my shoulders never to worry about paying for medical costs. I didn't feel the pinch until I had two more kids here in the U.S. When I first moved here I thought it was very fair. I paid a ten-dollar co-pay. Now everything costs more and our insurance covers less.

You can really see the pros and cons of both systems. Which would you say is preferable?

L: I don't want the Canadian system, but I do want something.

I can only comment on the health system in Quebec because every province runs differently.

When my mom has gotten sick, I've had to fly up there and kick butt to get doctors to do something. Her flu turned into pneumonia and the pneumonia got worse and worse. She would pass out and nearly died. I had to fly up there and yell at doctors. They are so behind there. It's federal dollars, it's not for profit. Up there a lot of times a doctor's salary is capped and they don't get paid after a certain number of patients. Up there the government is the insurance company.

Here the medical system is for profit, so guess what? They're going to do a good job as best they can and I get to pick my doctors. But people are going bankrupt here to pay for healthcare if they get cancer, or get really sick; it's ridiculous. It should not be that way. When I get a bill from the hospital it's funny money numbers. One of my kids needed stitches on his knee and the children's hospital charged twenty-five dollars for a band-aid. That is ridiculous.

The one thing the Canadian government got right is they tell the doctors and the hospitals what something should cost. That's why people are buying drugs in Canada. They're not making these companies go bankrupt—they're still making a profit, but it's not a ridiculous profit.

When you and someone else would go to a doctor in Quebec for the exact same treatment, did you have to pay more if you had more income?

L: No. When you go to the doctor or to the hospital you don't pay anything. I got a percentage taken out of my income to cover it, but if you're low income they don't take anything out of your income....so it's great to be poor in Quebec.

Back to before, all of those kids from the large French

families, many didn't go on to have any kids at all. There has been a large population drop in Quebec, so the government has brought in immigrants, but French-loving immigrants who will go to French schools and speak French, but they're not "pure lin;" they're not pure wool. This has been another backfire. Most of the immigrants who applied for Quebec have French backgrounds and are from former French colonies like Lebanon, Iran, and Egypt. A lot of them know how to speak French, but a lot of them are Muslim, and extreme Muslim. So the women are covered up in burqas. The Muslim population in Quebec is really high so the racist stuff starts coming out. About a year ago they even made a law that Muslim women covered up must uncover their faces. That's an actual new law.

How do you think your life would be different if you had been born in the United States? And/or how different are your children's lives having been raised here?

L: Overall it seems like Canadians are more people loving. Americans are all about "me."

I do feel my kids are not as worldly. People in Canada tend to travel more and are exposed to more cultures. Here we identify first as "Americans." In Canada people don't call themselves Canadian. Either you're Greek, or Israeli, or Vietnamese, or Jewish from Russia…We don't go by Canadian first. Everyone holds on to their culture there. In Quebec, most people are only one generation from being immigrated.

How do you identify? You are so multi-layered.

JS: What Lin said next resembled what Teri said about her experiences of being a stranger in a strange land.

L: It's weird because even in Quebec I was always an out-

77

sider, even in my community.

Even the Chinese who spoke Cantonese discriminated against my family. Most of the Chinese there spoke Cantonese because they had emigrated from Hong Kong, which was an easier route to Canada as a British colony. We were in the minority because we spoke Mandarin. We couldn't even understand each other. If we went to a Chinese shop they yelled at us to speak in Cantonese. Even the food we ate was different. I never had sweet and sour sauce until I ate at a Chinese restaurant in Montreal.

You still felt more accepted by the liberals in your community, though?

L: I actually felt most comfortable with my Jewish friends in Montreal. Most of them got out, though, and moved to California.

Why didn't your parents leave too?

L: Because they paid so long into the system. They were ideal citizens; they worked hard, and they never tried to cheat anything. So they thought they could finally retire and not worry about medical costs, but it's been a huge letdown because the medical system in Quebec is now imploding.

They can't afford to pay for all the baby boomers getting older who paid into the system. They used to have a cap on doctors' patients, but now they're letting them charge for more services so doctors love getting new patients now.

My dad was told he needed a colonoscopy. He was told, "You can either wait eight months and have an intern do it or you can pay me $250 and I can schedule you next week with an experienced doctor, which would be me."

Do you ever think, "I see where socialized medicine can go" when the topic is brought up for the United States?

L: The U.S. medical system does need to be fixed. It's gotten greedy. It's all about shareholders and profits. Who's going to set the prices? I don't know, but I don't want to see what's happened in Canada either.

Canada is trying to copy the English now. Canada is big on everyone's equal, but they're realizing there's abuse because of human nature. Just like not every doctor works because they love to heal people. The same for education. The government used to subsidize medical school, so it wasn't expensive. I went to Waterloo for my architecture degree. I went to school for four months, then worked for four months. It took six years to graduate, but I had two years of work under my belt. It was wonderful. Many of the universities are on that co-op system now. It was a good balance.

Are you a working architect?

L: I stopped when my third baby was born. In Texas you can have a comfortable life living on one income. There is no income tax and the cost of living is low. Groceries are dirt cheap compared to Canada. In Canada a lot of the produce is seasonal. In winter you're eating cabbage and carrots. Here I can have mangoes, fresh food, whenever I want. It's cheap because it all comes from Mexico.

It comes back to money and capitalism. Money drives society here. I cannot deny that. I cannot say I don't enjoy it. I am benefiting from it. I know what it is like not to have it.

Which issues that politicians talk about are most important to you?

L: The Democrats go on about universal healthcare and free college. I had that. You can't say it won't be a burden. We also have a lot richer people in the U.S., the super-rich. Whenever anyone gets rich in Canada they get out of there. Celine Dion is from Montreal. We have mutual friends we grew up with. When many people who worked with her got rich, Justin Bieber…they move to the States.

Which candidates are appealing to you?

L: I like people who can back up what they say with facts. I like Elizabeth Warren. She's smart. I like smart women. I'm watching Kamala Harris. She actually lived in Montreal for a while.

I'm still trying to reconcile how you are against some of the progressive candidates' policies, yet like the progressive candidates.

L: I think Democrats are under the bigger umbrella. Republicans are more selective about who can be under their umbrella…they're more like mean girls. Plus, pro-gun stuff drives me crazy.

You mentioned a turning point, when you decided you wanted to become a U.S. citizen, was after the 2000 election?

L: I had just moved here. I thought Gore was very educated. In Canada we usually vote for the more educated person. Gore had the numbers. It was ridiculous that he didn't win.

Political campaigns are also much shorter in Canada, about six months. Here it drags on for years. It gets to the point where it dulls us. We're over informed. And again, it goes back to money, money, who has the most money. You just want to shut it all off. That's what drives me crazy here.

Do you get involved in politics? Do you campaign?

L: No. I don't give my money to candidates or political causes —I'd rather give my money to, say, a children's hospital. I think the process is crazy here and don't want to contribute to that. It's true that in America you need money to win elections. I can't say I'm not enjoying it though.

Chapter 3

"A Child During the War"
Liz

"Transcends Politics"
Wally

Liz

"A Child During the War"

Born—1930 in Detroit, Michigan
Political Identity—Independent, but Leans
Republican

Liz was born at the beginning of the Great Depression, which shaped her in many ways during her formative years, not least of which to appreciate the small things, even a tossed penny, an attitude she carries with her to this day. "I think I just started life as conservative," Liz said several times during our conversations, a reminder that she represents those Americans who came of age during World War II, witnesses to the sacrifices that the country made as a whole.

Liz recalled a collective patriotism that carried America in years of struggle, first during World War II and then during Vietnam. The oldest of four children noted that most of the boys around her age went on to serve in the military from the end of World War II through the time of the Korean War, including her two younger brothers. "An attitude of country over party translated to how people treated one another too," Liz explained. She longs for the kind of unity in America that she said comes during shared hardship and believes that many of the problems that the country faces today stem from people not wanting to sacrifice.

Only a few months after we wrapped our interview, I thought of Liz when the novel coronavirus COVID-19 became a war Americans fought together. As our society of increased convenience was humbled, a roll of toilet paper a valued commodity, a long phone conversation during quarantine a luxury, I wondered if these were the kinds of things Liz meant when she underscored one of the paradoxes of war. While no one actually wants war, Liz explained how generations of Americans alive today are too far removed from it.

I was struck by what Liz had to say about the difference between the slow way news was circulated eighty years ago compared to the instantaneous way we get news today. From not knowing about the atrocities that were occurring in Europe, to what, exactly, was going on in that tropical place called Vietnam, while listening to Liz I couldn't help but think that the old way of getting the news sheltered people, which can be a benefit and a drawback.

When asked about her earliest political shaping memory, Liz launched into a story about her father coming home from work with a black eye. Before supermarkets were super-sized, Liz's father was a wholesale meat distributor, selling to butchers and small grocers. On the day Liz remembered, allegedly it was one of union leader Jimmy Hoffa's men who roughed up her father in his Detroit shop.

L: I was very young and remember Daddy coming home beaten up very badly by goon squads. It was terrible to see him like that. Up until then, unions hadn't been prominent in our life. We thought of those men as less union than as a group of gang members who wanted my dad to use their truck. My dad paid the consequences when he said no.

Did that experience make you feel anti-union?

L: No, because on the other hand my husband of sixty years was in the white-collar union, TOPS (Technical Office Professional Workers), which gave us and our three children a wonderful life.

JS: Liz has been widowed since 2014.

Do you remember feeling fearful during the Depression and later the war?

L: I didn't feel fear. Daddy had a good job, and everyone was patriotic. That's what I miss most. Today there is no respect for law or order; it's every man for himself.

Why do you think that is?

L: I think it's because after the war everything was good. The soldiers came home, got jobs, got married, and had kids. Everybody was happy and proud. When you heard the Star-Spangled Banner, you would get chills. There was a feeling of patriotism and of feeling proud. But this has changed in the last fifteen years.

So, you believe our society has been patriotic up until fifteen years ago? Even during the Vietnam War?

L: Yes. Sure, I was disappointed in people at times; things were not always perfect, but you see, when we were growing up, we never heard about the Third World. We didn't grow up with that geography. Vietnam was a place far, far away. They were just starting to send cruise ships there.

It wasn't until kids started coming home from Vietnam and you heard stories that we understood what was happening. My neighbor's husband came home deaf from being beaten so severely. When we got more information and talked with people we started to hear about the cruel treatment of our soldiers, which banded us together.

It's a reminder that you didn't get news right away like we do now.

L: Oh yes. Unlike today, where we get news in a heartbeat, back then it would take at least two days before any news reached us.

How long did it take to learn about what Hitler was doing in Europe? When did you learn the full story of the Holocaust?

L: When we first starting hearing things it was like, "That can't be for real! They wouldn't be doing that!"

But I knew it was true sooner than most people my age because I had a firsthand source. I had a Jewish girlfriend who I knew through Girl Scouts and her grandparents were killed by the Nazis. Her name was Marcy. Her parents had moved with her to America from Austria several years before the war started; they had just felt uneasy being over there and left their families to come to America.

Marcy told me a story about when she still lived in Austria. She and her mother were walking down the street one day and Marcy let out a scream because it looked like dozens of bodies were floating down the Danube River. They were mannequins from Jewish merchants' shops! It started with Nazis destroying Jewish merchants' businesses by destroying their property. This was just at the start of what would eventually come.

Marcy's parents kept trying to call home to Austria. It was quite a challenge back then to make a long-distance call like that. You would call the operator and the operator would call back like six hours later saying if she could reach the person or not. Sometimes Marcy's parents would try calling for several days and I remember how worried they were. One day, someone in her grandparents' building happened to answer the phone and said the grandparents had been taken away during the night. That's how they found out. Marcy's parents told her that her grandparents had been taken to the camp. No one fully knew at the time what that meant, but her grandparents were never heard from again.

No, we certainly didn't hear about news like we do now. It was the same when Pearl Harbor was bombed. I was at the Detroit Institute of Art in the mummy room and a security guard asked us if we'd heard what had happened. My parents had no idea.

Do you remember what it was like to be a child during World War II?

L: I remember the rationing. I missed that we couldn't go on our Sunday car rides anymore because our gas was rationed. We traded our gas stamps to get a couple of pounds of butter. There was a store at the end of the street where the owner would give us butter and we would give him our gas. Then daddy would bring home meat and we would give the meat to neighbors and they'd give us their gas rationing. Rationing was very interesting. It taught so many of us self-control and how to appreciate things. To this day, having to ration made it so that I will still stop to pick up a coin; that copper penny is worth money! My children and grandchildren like to tease me for this, but I've thought that way since I was a young girl.

During the war, I remember that my job was to take the paper off of every aluminum can and then I had to flatten it so that it could be turned in for metal. I also remember that my grandmother donated her Persian lamb coat to the war efforts so that the pilots could have warm jackets going up into the air.

We valued things very strongly back then, very strongly. I always had to work for an allowance. I had to clean every baseboard in the whole house every Saturday morning. Once a month I had to take the crystals off of our chandelier and clean them with vinegar and baking soda. To this day, whenever I see dirty baseboards, I remember how that was my job and I want to clean them.

Are there any issues right now that you think should be prioritized?

L: I am concerned with pro-life issues. I'll go along with abortion up to three months, but I think partial birth abortion is plain infanticide. It is plain wrong. If a woman doesn't know by the time she's ready to give birth that she doesn't want the baby, don't murder the baby. This issue is especially important to me because I have two adopted special needs grandchildren who deserve to be on this earth.

At least someone who wants assisted suicide has to have a sane mind to choose it. But it doesn't make sense that assisted suicide could be illegal, while it's legal to take an innocent baby who doesn't have a choice and murder it. If it's right for one, why isn't it right for both?

I am pro-death penalty, however. I know that sooner or later someone will get a 'death sentence who is innocent, but after being on death row for eighteen years, someone will figure it out if they shouldn't be there.

I also highly disagree with this new idea of some candidates wanting to give people a free college education. If someone wants to cut costs, they can go to a community college for one-tenth the cost and get the first two years of college out of the way before transferring. If a student survives and does well those two years, I think then give them some help through financial aid.

As an Independent, have you gravitated more toward either party?

L: I have voted for both Democrats and Republicans. I think not allowing Independents to vote in primaries is so wrong. The primaries are the most important elections we have because that is when we determine the best people. Other than the primary I can vote for who I want, and I stay involved by working at the polls during elections.

I've always been Independent, but I think now I'm a Republican. I can't afford to be a Democrat any longer.

Why is that?

L: I feel Republicans stand for pulling yourself up from your bootstrap versus Democrats who I think believe in being given things. I think the Democratic Party has really shifted more to this attitude of, if you don't want to work, well they just give it to you. I believe we have to work for what we want and for what we get, and we aren't supposed to expect somebody to give it to us. Nobody ever gave me anything except my mom and dad. I resent the inference that people can just ask for it and they get things. These days it seems people don't even have to ask for it; things are just sent to them.

I worked for forty-eight years. Why should I have to hand

over my money to somebody who doesn't want to work? God knows there's enough of them.

JS: Liz was a homemaker until her youngest of three children turned nine, at which time she worked part-time, always in jobs related to customer service.

L: The Democrats also have all these movie stars that they're relying on for decisions. Where does an actor or an actress get off knowing how I feel? Do they know what's going on right now, south of Eight Mile? Meryl Streep is a wonderful actress, but what gives her any clout politically? Just because they have a famous name, it doesn't mean they are a role model. Since the general public doesn't read anymore, they take any celebrity or someone with a famous name and suddenly they become a wiz in many subjects. That upsets me.

JS: Today Liz is active, swimming nearly every day and she volunteers ten hours a week at a hospital.

L: I help get patients ready for blood work and x-rays and I train the kids who come in to volunteer. We have a hard time finding volunteers because it's hard to find young people who will give of themselves like that. They don't want to work for an hour, let alone four hours. They're coming in for community service hours and all I hear is, "I'm tired. I want a break."

Or, "What do you mean? I'm supposed to do this for no pay?"

"I have to leave an hour early. I have a date with my girlfriend."

They don't know what work is. I blame my generation for this.

Why do you blame your generation?

L: Because we came out of the war and everything was good, so we gave our kids every comfort. And then they did the same for their kids. They've never experienced real want before in their lives and I think this has been damaging to our country.

Wally
"Transcends Politics"

Born—1923 in Inglewood, California
Political Identity—Conservative
Republican

Wally symbolizes the generation of people that developed grit on the other end of hardship, who put country over party, and who would never get used to just passing by a nickel in the corner of a sidewalk. Like Liz (A Child During the War), one of Wally's guiding beliefs is that self-esteem can only come from hard work and struggle. He thinks one reason that so many people are less happy today, despite more creature comforts, is a lack of grit. Wally expressed these feelings, like Liz, shortly before our country was hit by COVID-19. In the way communities rallied, reaching out to the most vulnerable and heralding our front line in this invisible war, our medical workers, I got an inkling of what Wally meant when he said, "Struggle offers opportunity for growth."

Yet reaching his hand out to others, literally, is central to who Wally is. At times while interviewing Wally I had to pull the conversation back to politics because, I learned, Wally transcends politics. While he is clear on why he votes for Republican issues and candidates, it was clear to me that most of Wally's political shaping stories are metaphors for something bigger than politics— humanity. Politics are merely his starting point.

When asked about his earliest political shaping memory, Wally started where it all began, even before his birth, with his parents' meeting. Wally's father owned a theater in New York and his mother came to work there as an actress. The newlyweds made their way west to California during the early years of film, when the allure of fame beckoned many in theater to take their shot on a much larger, gilded stage. However, Wally's parents' dream would sputter before it even got started. Upon arriving in Los Angeles, Wally's mother "took one look" and said, "This isn't for us, Frank." With a young family to support, Wally's father turned to insurance. Wally would be the fourth child of five born to the couple. (His twin sister would claim the number three title by minutes.)

Wally celebrated his sixth birthday just days before the Stock Market Crash of October 1929, a cataclysmic event that would have devastating consequences for the global economy, the ripple effects of which would herald in the Great Depression.

"The first thing people cut was their insurance policies," Wally recalled. "They couldn't afford it."

Their income slashed, the family of seven lost their home. They packed up and moved an hour east to more affordable San Bernardino, California where they found a home to live in for ten dollars a month.

Do you remember what that was like?

W: That time was really crushing to my mother, but we never missed a meal...never. I don't know how she did it.

JS: Wally recalled the term "hobo", a common term at that time to describe a traveling worker without a home. Wally only had to look out his front door, which was near a railroad track, to see how others struggled too.

"There was a Hobo Camp right there," he said, vividly recalling groups of men hovering around a single pot at meal times, using a can to scoop "slumgullion," a meager soup made with whatever could be found, but usually turnips and potatoes.

His mother continued to stretch the family's withering resources.

W: We didn't have much, but my mother would never turn anyone down. If someone came looking for something to eat, she'd say, "Stay out here on the porch and I'll find you something."

Everything was always used; nothing was ever thrown away. My mother was so upset but she kept at it, whatever it was.

JS: Although a homemaker, out of necessity she found work to supplement the family's income like picking seasonal apricots and painting black-and-white photographs with color.

Wally remembered feeling tugged toward self-reliance, a conviction that would continue to deepen throughout his life. He explained how he never felt sorry for himself or felt like anyone else had better circumstances than his own.

W: Everyone was in the same boat...In fact, many people did not have a home. People traveled by train by the thousands to find whatever work they could.

JS: Among different jobs to "earn a few bucks", Wally had a paper route and he sold magazines door to door. By the time he was twelve years old Wally bought his own clothes to help his parents, something that made him feel proud.

W: My parents impressed on me that we grow by the painful things. One of the best compliments was when my mother would say, "I'll never worry about Wally because he'll make it. I know he'll be able to take care of himself."

JS: As soon as he graduated from San Bernardino High School in 1941, Wally enlisted in the Navy, with the dream of becoming a Navy carrier pilot.

W: One look at me, and I don't know how serious people took me. I was a one-hundred-twenty-three-pound kid. Still, I've always believed, once you set a goal you hang on to that goal.

JS: Wally started out as a radio operator. He was a recent radio school graduate on December 7, 1941. He had been stationed at Ford Island and was among those in the first convoy to arrive after the bombing of Pearl Harbor. Like many veterans from his generation, Wally doesn't give many details about his time during the war, but he shared life lessons that he took away from his years in the service.

W: I learned that hate and anger get you nowhere. You hate these people and those people…Next thing you know it's the other way around and they can hate you just as easy. It's all relative, but the hate and anger are still there.

Did you believe in the war efforts?

W: I've always been a freedom fighter. That's the way I am. I believed in what we were doing because we were fighting for a cause, but I learned early on that you can fight for freedom, but you also have to have love and kindness.

JS: While he worked as a radio operator, Wally also worked on combat airplanes.

W: Every job I took I had to be the best, you know, and they noticed it. I knew what I wanted to do. I wanted to be the best sailor the Navy ever had. Energy follows thought; you have to have the thought.

JS: When he asked to be transferred his commanding officer didn't want to let him go, but offered Wally a challenge—if he could log 200 hours in a patrol plane, then he could transfer to aircraft work. On his days off, Wally did just that.

W: When I went to flight school, well that changed everything. Five years later I was doing slow rolls over my high school in the fastest fighter plane the Navy had. I went all the way down to the South Pacific in a fighter plane.

JS: Wally went on to fly seventy-two missions during the Berlin Blockade and Korean War. After twenty years and one month in the Navy, Wally retired as a Lieutenant Commander.

W: Eight more months and I would have retired as a full commander, but by then I didn't feel it was fair to my wife and four kids.

What were some of the things that shaped you during that time?

W: You destroy things. I was dropping one thousand pound bombs, but at the end of the day we were fighting for freedom. During the Korea Conflict we were fighting to save the freedom of the South Koreans, but look at what's still happening today—North Korea is still trying to destroy South Korea. After all this time, there is still the hate and anger...it's still there.

JS: After the Korea Conflict, Wally was stationed in Hawaii. After being active Navy for ten years he stayed in the Naval Reserves for ten years. With his flying experience Wally worked as a pilot for United Airlines for thirty years, a memory that still brings a smile.

W: This is your captain speaking...I would stand in the door and I could tell that people liked to have me say goodbye to them. Do you know that the word goodbye is actually a contraction of a little English prayer, meaning "God be with you?" So, when you're saying goodbye to someone you're really saying, "God be with you."

If someone says goodbye to you, you should say, "Thank you for the blessing." Tell them what it means.

JS: About fifteen years ago, while out on his daily walk, Wally was reminded how much a greeting and a simple wave might turn someone's day from bad to good. Known first as the neighborhood greeter, Wally began waving to morning commuters and kids walking to school. Then he added fist bumps and has since added inspirational sayings, including, "Be kind whenever possible," and, "The only time you look down on someone is when you're helping them up."

In the years since, Wally has made it his mission to connect with as many people as possible, which he says fuels him just as much as it does them.

W: Soon the principal told me he could see a positive change happening with how students were interacting at school. Apparently, it was working and I didn't even know it. We're trying to get the ripple effect going. Energy follows thought and love is the same.

JS: Politics is just the tip of the iceberg to Wally—a cover for deeper ideas. When we talked about the current partisan divide in America, Wally went into a discussion about energy pathways, astrology, the Age of Aquarius, and more, surprising to me to hear from a man of his generation.

W: You can expect to see a degeneration of our country, but that's okay because it's part of God's plan. You always tear yourself down before you are brought back up, even your own body. It will be a long time before we get back. There's going to be an axis change that comes along and changes everything. Opposing factions, like what we have today with the Democrat and Republican parties, always play a role.

It's surprising that you talk about energy pathways and such. How did this come to be?

W: I've always been very intuitive-I've been meditating since I was nine. I love people and animals, all things that grow. I don't even like to fish. I gave up fishing because I don't need to fish for food. When you see a fish gasping...well, that's a living thing...

How do you think the tone of this country has changed since the 1950s? Do you believe we have we evolved as a society?

W: No, I don't think so. I thought so in the 1950s when we came back from Korea. Things were starting to change. The stuff the people were intent on changing was like breaking new ground. We were getting the soil ready for the new age coming and we are in that age right now—The Age of Aquarius, which came in the mid-1950s. But then Vietnam was a disaster and once China was lost to the Communists it was pretty sad. From that time on things started going from bad to worse. We've had nothing but pain ever since. The men who came home from Vietnam still have scars that won't quit.

There's going to be an axis change that comes along and changes everything. Look at the pyramids and Atlantis. Look at the role of opposing factions in all of this; again, it is like what we have today with the Democrat and Republican Parties.

This country is going down the tubes as it is today. We've made a lot of mistakes, but Vietnam was one of the worst as far as karma. And before that it was how we treated American Indians. You can expect to see a degeneration of our country, but that's okay because it's part of God's plan. It will be a long time before we get back to stability.

When Nixon was President the same thing was going on. It was not good for our country. Nixon had to learn humility. We have to learn all sides. That's why there are twelve signs of the Zodiac. Things change. You could be a brilliant physician and return as a hobo or a drunk just to learn what it's like, the other side of the coin. There are painful lessons to learn but that's where you get your growth. This too shall pass. By the time it passes, some people commit suicide because they can't handle it. I've had my share of pain during and after the war, but I got over it. Suffering makes you think about other people. Look at Jesus, for instance. He died in pain.

What do you think has changed most about society?

W: Attitudes. People with attitudes. It starts at our colleges and with our professors. They are preaching the wrong things. They should be preaching honesty and they should keep out of politics, just like the NFL. We had season tickets for seventeen years for the '49ers but stopped going after the kneeling controversy.

Politics has changed for the worse; it didn't used to be like this. I think the worst part is political correctness. It rankles everybody; now everybody's racist.

When I grew up, I had five rules of thumb that I passed on to my kids and now the kids who I see in my community. My five rules of thumb are, don't smoke, don't drink, don't take drugs, don't use profanity, and don't become promiscuous. Some kids today are jumping in the sack with whoever comes along. When they're ready to settle down, the real meaning of love is gone. It's not for me to judge. "Judge and you shall be judged," but if they don't commit themselves to marriage, then the first blow up they have, they walk out.

JS: Wally has been married for sixty-two years and has four children and five grandchildren.

What's the secret to a long marriage?

W: You have to learn to let bygones be bygones.

What are some of the other Wally-isms you tell young people?

W: I tell kids, "You can either be articulate or profane, but you can't be both."

I also tell them to select their friends very carefully in high school, because when they hit sixteen everything changes.

Of all the things you tell kids, what is the most important?

W: Start to think love and kindness in everything you do. Stop thinking hate and anger toward people. Never look down on anyone unless you're helping them up. Live in a way that those who know you but don't know God will learn to know God because they know you.

What issues make you align with the Republican party?

W: I believe strongly in The Constitution and the Bill of Rights. I feel this is the main difference between the Democratic and Republican parties. The conservative party believes in the Constitution as it was written. We have a very strong Constitution written by geniuses who could see far into the future. Today they are trying to change it. For example, many on the Democratic side are trying to do away with the Electoral College and decide elections based on the popular vote. If we did that, then large cities would decide elections.

I know we've had a lot of lousy candidates on the Republican side, but I still think the principles are more about helping make your own life better instead of waiting for someone to do it for you.

Have you always voted Republican?

W: Always. I am a conservative. I believe a person has to earn his keep if he can. You have to strive to be your own person. If you're taking dole from this person and that person, it's difficult to do that. Some people need help at times, but I think that God put us down here to learn, to strive, and to grow.

Chapter 4

"His Mother's Son"
Chuck

"The Nostalgic Observer"
Alice

Chuck
"His Mother's Son"

Born—1943 in Louisville, Kentucky
Political Identity—Independent

Chuck was raised in the South during segregation. The oldest of four children never knew his father, but Chuck said his mother filled that void and beyond. At ninety-three years old, she continues to be Chuck's greatest role model and the two talk on the phone nearly every day. It's not hyperbole to say that Chuck is in awe of his mother, attributing all of his shaping, politically and otherwise, to her.

Chuck recalled that while growing up, Wednesday night was a highlight of the week. "All the black people got together at Grace Community Center for a potluck," he recalled. "The kids played basketball and boxed. No one knew who was poor. We just got together and ate."

One potluck in particular stands out to Chuck. It was 1955 and at the end of the night a crowd swarmed around a thirteen-year-old Cassius Clay, Louisville's most famous former resident. But in 1955 the boy who went on to become the most famous boxer in the world, changing his name during the Vietnam War to Muhammad Ali, was a year older than Chuck and the source of some athletic envy.

"Cassius got six or seven awards during that award ceremony and I got two," Chuck explained. "I turned to my mother and said, 'Why did he get so many?'"

"Because he out-loved you, Charles Edward," she said. "He made more friends than you.'"

It was a moment Chuck wouldn't forget. He told his mom right then, "I want to be like that."

At nineteen Chuck left Louisville for the Army. It was once the Vietnam veteran was stationed in San Francisco that he met his wife, to whom he has been married for fifty years. He became an insurance agent, and together the couple raised two sons in the Bay Area. It was while raising his family that politics first entered his consciousness.

While growing up, politics was something out of reach, accessible, seemingly to Chuck, to the rich and powerful. Fellow church members gravitated toward Chuck's magnetic personality. They encouraged him to get involved in local politics. Chuck served on his city council and went on to become Solano County's first black mayor. When asked how a non-politician could do the job, Chuck said it was precisely because he wasn't a politician.

Like Wally (Transcends Politics), Chuck is passionate about the state of the nation and the world, and does what he can to affect change in his own sphere of influence. Like Wally, the passing years have offered Chuck time for reflection. His politics are less rigid, more human.

What is your earliest political shaping memory?

C: I had never, ever registered to vote. I never bothered because I always felt like everybody else was going to do what they wanted to do anyway. It wasn't until I was thirty-six years old and a Sunday school superintendent that I gave it any thought. Some church members, my pastor, and my deacon, said, "Why don't you get into politics? You'd be great here in town." That's really what inspired me.

So when you were a child, were politics ever brought up?

C: The only thing we knew about politics was that somebody would stop by during election time and leave political literature and say, "Okay, tell your mom that this is what we're going to do and we need her vote."

And that was it. They never asked us what we wanted. That really turned me off. I thought, "Why do I want to be bothered with this?" If you're running for something, ask people what they want.

JS: Chuck would become his county's first black mayor, serving between 1993 and 1997.

Were you a Democrat or a Republican Mayor?

C: There was no party affiliation and I liked that. In the mid-2000s we moved to be closer to my wife's job. I was a registered Democrat, but discovered I was living in totally Republican territory. A guy told me, "I don't know if you want to go out as a Democrat, you may want to switch."

I said, "Well I can't do Republican," so I switched to an Independent, which I am right now.

Why couldn't you consider being a Republican? Do you vote along party lines?

C: I'd say that now I vote for the person. I go with my heart and the way that I feel. I can say now that if a candidate is a Republican, that's where I go. If he's a Democrat, that's where I go. If I feel good about someone, then that's where I'm going to go.

The last thing I want is for somebody running for office to say, "Well, I didn't vote for such and such because I'm a Republican." That's the worst thing you could tell me. You just lost my vote. I mean, if something comes down that you don't like, you have to look in the mirror. I'm going to vote my conscience and if that means a Republican, so be it.

JS: Chuck's role as a youth sports coach for more than forty years has also been influential when it comes to shaping his politics; how he sees the world. Chuck was inspired to coach by his own youth sports coach and former director of Grace Community Center, Freddie Stoner. Chuck credits Stoner with impressing upon him what it means to be confident and "the greatest," words that were signature to Muhammad Ali, whom Stoner mentored as well.

C: I never forgot it. Freddie used to tell us, "You can be as good as anybody or better," and, "If they can do it, so can you."

How did this motivation translate into how you were as a coach and as a politician?

C: Coming up I always said to myself, "How can I get better?" Well I learned to be a better listener. That is really what works for me. I don't make the mistake of telling people what they should do. Instead, I've got to be an active listener and I've got to love more people. It's as simple as that.

And I tell the kids that I coach, "Don't try to be anything that you're not. Just take whatever you have and develop that. Learn to love someone and learn to listen." And I can tell you, that's it. That's the secret to my success, if you want to call it that. If I were to go back and run for mayor again, I think I'd win because people trusted me.

How was it getting into politics when you weren't a politician?

C: It was great because every time the press came to talk to me, I had to be on the ball. I really had to have it together. And that's what encouraged me. One of the best compliments was when a reporter told me I would always answer the tough questions and I liked when people told me I was accessible. All you have to do is be yourself. Be who you are and be honest, and you can make it.

How have you seen politics change in your lifetime, for good or for bad?

C: Well, you know, what I've noticed is a lot of guys, women or whoever, get into politics for the glory of themselves, not for the glory of us, the people. That bothers me. And all you have to do is listen; just keep your mouth shut and listen.

My mom really emphasized the power of words to me. My mom is my best friend forever. She's never steered me wrong. She always kept me in the Bible. One day she said, "I want you to read the Book of James. It tells you about controlling your tongue. You can really hurt people by not controlling your tongue and you can really help people by saying the right thing. Watch what you say."

She's absolutely right.

How did being the oldest of four kids shape you?

C: Because my mom raised four of us by herself, and by me being the oldest, I had to take the lead. So I had to get the job and that type of thing, but I enjoyed that. I enjoyed the responsibility. It was quite challenging, but I said to myself, "Hey, I'm the head of the household. I've got to do it."

Do you think that was intrinsically inside of you to be motivated like that? Where did that come from?

C: My mother…she's everything to me. I mean, I cannot even describe what she means to me. When you look in the dictionary to find what *greatness* is, it still does not describe my mother to a tee. I mean, she is *it*.

Someone asked me one day, "What would your greatest wish be?" My greatest wish would be to die before my mother dies. I couldn't deal with that. I mean, she's just, she's unbelievable. She came up with answers that we thought were impossible to answer. She's just it. She's totally it.

That's beautiful. I can't imagine greater words to hear from your child.

C: *She* is beautiful.

Did you ever give your mom any grief?

C: Oh, all the time.

Your dad was not in your life when you were growing up. How did that influence you?

C: Yeah. That's why I've enjoyed coaching for so many years. Kids can't come to me with any special problem that I haven't faced before. A lot of them were being raised by their mothers. I told them they can't tell me they got in trouble because their dad wasn't home. I told them right away, "My dad wasn't there and look what happened to me."

Once I tell them that, you see the frown go to a smile. I always tell my kids, "If Coach can do it, so can you."

JS: Chuck requires that his players have good grades, clean their rooms, tell their parents they love them every day and they must high-five him every time they see him.

That's always the hope that someone without a father can still turn out to be a great father. Is it really all because of your mother? You give her all the credit?

C: Absolutely.

What is your stance on the Black Lives Matter movement?

C: If you print nothing else, print this. If people trust you, they will help you. And if people trust you, they will listen to you. And this is one of the problems that we have right now. You look at what's going on now; people are not listening. That's where you have your problems. But if somebody listens to you and trusts you, it is going to work out.

Do you think it's important for black men to see more police officers who look like them? Is that who they will identify with and trust?

C: Absolutely. When I was the mayor our city manager came to me one day and said, "You know what? We need some more police officers."

And with me coaching, I knew how to get an answer right away. Go to the kids. They're going to tell you the truth. And I went out one day and had my basketball practice and said, "Hey guys, I need a question answered. Our city manager thinks we need more police officers, and I do, too. But I want to see what you guys think."

We had this little kid who is now a big-time police lieutenant and he said, "Coach. So, I think it'd be good, but if somebody is going to hit me upside the head with a bullet, I want him to look like me."

I said, "Right on."

And that's what we did. We hired Hispanics. We hired whites, blacks. It was great because you came into my town and I wanted you to see what we're about, reflected right there in our police department.

The conversation doesn't stay centered on political parties with you. Is that accurate?

C: Yes. I was watching television recently and there was a black CEO on. He said, "Here it is the twenty-first century, and we're going back fifty years and we're still trying to solve the same problem."

But it's easy; it's absolutely easy. If you are giving and you're not insecure, it can work. We don't have to have the struggles we're seeing now. If we could get rid of the word *insecure*, so many problems would disappear.

Yes. I think that's true with a lot of things actually, the secret to a happy marriage too.

C: Yeah, I totally agree. When my sons brought home my future daughters-in-law my sons knew what I expected. I love that I got two of the greatest daughters-in-law in the history of daughters-in-law and five beautiful grandkids. My grandkids, as soon as we talk, they say, "Paw Paw, before you ask me, my grades are great."

They know what I expect. So I'm telling you, let people see that you love them, and watch what happens.

It sounds like local politics mean more to you, touching the people that you can actually see and interact with, than national politics. Would you say that's right?

C: That's exactly right. When you plant a seed, you put it in the ground; it starts from the beginning. I don't want a plant that's already fully developed. I want to develop that plant myself. To plant a lawn, you start by tilling the soil and putting the seed in the ground and watching it grow. As it comes up and needs clipping, you clip it. When it needs watering, you water it. Life is so simple. Why do we make it complicated?

That's very wise. What do you think our country needs right now?

C: Our country needs leadership and it needs more love and compassion. And that comes in all forms, all colors. Nobody can come to me and say, "Hey I want you to help this white boy because he's white," or "I want you to help this black guy because he's black." I couldn't care less about that. Where is his heart? Where is her heart? That's where I'm coming from. Do you have a heart? Do you want to help?

What did you think when you experienced bigoted behavior in your lifetime?

JS: Chuck smiled warmly.

C: Coming back to my mom again…growing up in Louis-ville, the heart of the south. Let me tell you, a lot of problems. I remember one day I came in the house and I was crying. My mother said, "What's wrong?"

I said, "That man called me a nigger."

My mom was quiet for a minute. She said, "Baby, can I tell you something?"

I said, "Yeah."

She said, "I want you to get the word *understand* in your vocabulary. You have to understand where people are coming from. And if you understand that, you will be okay."

I never forgot that, I never forget it. And I mean, I was mad. I mean, this guy was one of the most hated guys in the neighborhood because he preyed on making people mad and calling people names. He was kind of prominent, so he got away with it.

And that's when I respected my mom even more.

Did that sully your impression of people who had positions of power? Did you set out to be a leader who was antithetical to that?

C: Absolutely. In fact, we had a situation. We were getting ready to pass a Mello-Roos and man, everybody came out of the woodwork because they didn't want another tax. And we had this one guy that came to every council meeting to tell us why he didn't want to have the tax. One day I asked him to meet me for coffee.

Just by sitting down and talking, he ended up becoming one of my biggest advocates. When people listen, it makes a big deal. All you got to do is be simple and love people.

Do you think it's important for kids of different races to have other kids at school who look like them?

C: I think it helps. But I'll tell you something. If you want to grow, you've got to have tough skin.

I would grow up again in Louisville. It was one of the greatest things that ever happened to me.

You were growing up during segregation. What do you remember about that time?

C: Back to my mom again...I went to Male High School, but that's where all the white kids went. The black kids, including Muhammad Ali, went to Central High School. I was supposed to go to Central, all the black kids were supposed to. I came in the house one day and my mom said, "Hey, you're going to Male next year."

I said, "That's where all the white kids go."

And she said, "That's why you're going."

I was adamant. I didn't want to go.

Why then was it a great experience for you?

C: Because my mom wanted to challenge me; she knew I was smart. She said, "I've got to make it tough for him" because a lot of times kids who are smart, their parents make it too easy on them. My mom always made me work for it. I was mad, but I'll tell you, going to Male was one of the greatest experiences of my life. It made me grow.

What percentage of students were white?

C: Oh, ninety percent. Male High School had a little money, very ritzy. I remember one day, I'll never forget this guy who was also black. Now he is a professor at one of the top universities in the country. I was wearing the same pants for two weeks in a row. He came up to me one day and said,

119

"Charlie, when are you gonna change your pants? Because every time I look up, you got the same pants on."

That killed me. I couldn't say anything because he was standing there in front of some other people. I just kept my mouth shut and I went to class. I said to myself, "One of these days I'm going to make it better."

And it made me, it made me strong. It really did. And so I think if you put a child in a situation where he's got to grow, it helps. My mom put me in situations that were very challenging. She put me at Male, and I ended up doing well academically and everything, so I couldn't really be upset.

Many people say it's a mistake not to recognize skin color, but when I talk to you, I don't get that idea. How do you reconcile that?

C: I'd like to tell you something about what happened to one of my kids. My youngest son is forty-four years old now but when he started school forty years ago he met this little buddy. He came home all excited. He was telling me about this kid, but that he didn't know where he lived. I told him to tell me what his friend looks like. I asked him, "What color is he?"

"I don't know," my son said.

I eventually learned this friend is white, but isn't that nice that he said that he didn't know? That's what it should be about. The two of them are still best friends to this day.

I'm telling you right now, until we can get rid of the word *insecurity* we're not moving forward. It's simple. If you lead your life the right way, if you love and respect people the right way, you are going to get rewards that you've never, ever received.

In your lifetime, has there been a politician, whether it be a local or national leader, who you thought did a good job?

C: I like Obama. I think he did a fantastic job. When I was a mayor, I was impressed with Andrew Young. He was a black mayor of Atlanta (from 1982–1990).

What qualities did Obama and Young have that you thought were great in terms of being effective leaders?

C: Honesty and integrity. You've got to have that. You know, with me, you've got to be able to walk into a room and demand attention. You can't demand attention unless you give it.

One time a parent came up to me and said, "Coach, what's your ambition?"

I said, "Ma'am, I always want to be a hero to the kids." That's all I wanted to be when I was growing up. I just wanted to be a hero to the kids because the kids are our future.

The other day my wife comes in and I'm crying. She asked, "What happened?"

I said, "Remember this kid? He's getting ready to get his degree and he sent me this invitation…"

That's what it's about for me. I tell my kids, "You never know what they're going to say, but make sure they say something about you that's good."

Chuck with Muhammad Ali at a
Louisville event in the 1990s

Alice

"The Nostalgic Observer"
Born—1972 in Newark, New Jersey
Political Identity—Democrat

I talked with Alice two weeks after the killing of George Floyd. Captured on video, Floyd's murder while in Minneapolis Police custody brought global attention to the Black Lives Matter movement. At the time of our interview nightly protests were taking place in big and small cities across America, and the world. Alice, a black woman, is vocal about Black Lives Matter, but her thoughts on carrying forth its mission were not what I expected.

After talking with both Chuck (His Mother's Son) and Alice, I realized that I had entered both conversations assuming that they would have a lot to say about systemic racism because they are black, but also because it seemed everyone in America was talking about what systemic racism means. To my surprise, they didn't. My assumption served as another reminder, one of many, that continues to uphold this book's theme: Our individual political shaping stories are varied and nuanced. When we make sweeping generalizations about people because of their race, gender, age, religion, political affiliation, or something else (the list goes on), individual complexities, and therefore the truth, are lost. Instead, by taking the time to understand a person's shaping story before making judgments, we could drastically reduce, if not eliminate, the current partisan divide that threatens to rip this country apart.

When Alice was six years old a job transfer caused her and her parents to move from New Jersey to California. An only child, she settled into her new surroundings quickly, describing an idyllic childhood. Alice recalled playing outside until the streetlights came on, a reminder to head home. Like Chuck, Alice had a positive high school experience. She felt her high school was diverse enough that she never felt the shame that can come from standing out, particularly for children.

Now a single mother, Alice longs for her daughter to have the same carefree childhood that she had. The lens through which Alice sees the world is through that of a mother. Where Chuck idolizes his mother as the single strongest influence in his life, and she continues to fill that role well into her nineties, Alice is still in the thick of childrearing, striving to be the same source of strength and stability for her child.

Like many Americans, Alice gets much of her news about current events and politics on social media platforms like Facebook and her opinions often reflected this. Like Chuck and Wally (Transcends Politics), discussing politics with Alice mostly led her to make larger statements about society. Social issues are the heart of Alice's interest in politics.

From what you remember, why did you first identify as a Democrat?

A: I guess I was following in my parents' footsteps. They were Democrats so I always knew I would be a Democrat too.

Have you always voted since you were eighteen?

A: Oh, yes, I have.

Do you vote in local elections too?

A: I vote in all elections.

How was the importance of voting instilled in you?

A: I don't know about my mom, but my dad always voted. He took me with him to the polls. So when I had a kid, I planned to take my daughter to the polls so she could experience everything that goes on and, you know, I think she's more political than I am now.

JS: Alice laughed and continued to be energized whenever the subject turned to her daughter.

Did your dad ever explain why he felt it important to vote?

A: He did. He'd say to me, "You always have to have a voice."

Were there any candidates over the years that you liked more than any others, that you thought were good leaders?

A: Obama. I just really liked him and his wife. I liked how

(Michelle Obama) came out with, I think it was like, "no kid hungry." There were tanks of food and a program so that kids could have healthier meals.

(The Obamas) were a family, you know? He was involved in his girls' lives. He had his wife doing things...

So you liked the whole unit, the whole Obama family?

A: Yeah, exactly.

You live in Los Angeles. What do you think about living in California right now? Is there anything you would like to see change?

A: I'm ready to move...just everything that has been happening out here. You have riots and stuff. People are out protesting. Some are violent and some are not violent. It's just like, I don't want to raise my daughter in a place like this. I don't like where I'm raising her, not at all.

JS: While my next question was meant to be about her thoughts on the Black Lives Matter movement, Alice interpreted it to be about the coronavirus pandemic. At the time of our interview most states in the country were beginning to reopen after being essentially shuttered for three months.
Do you have an opinion about what's going on?

A: I think it's ridiculous that they're opening up all these places so soon. If you look at all of the news that's going on, the virus is escalating.

So your concerns stem from worry about catching the virus more so than worry from an economic standpoint?

A: I mean, people are hurting financially. Yeah, I get it. But, you know, I get all these e-mails and things saying that these places are hiring and that place is hiring. Then you apply and you don't get a call back. I'm unemployed and I apply for places every single day. It's discouraging.

Were you working up until the closures? Did you get laid off?

A: Yeah, I got laid off.

Do you want to say what your industry is?

A: It wasn't what I wanted to be doing, it was in, basically, telemarketing and I hated it. I want to get back in to working with kids or working with children or adults with disabilities. I loved it. That was my passion.

You mentioned you have a child. Do you want to share anything more about your family?

A: Yes, I have an almost fourteen-year-old daughter. She was diagnosed with ADHD, which is very difficult. We've had some rough times to the point where she was taken out of my home because she decided to destroy the house. And, you know, I call the police, but *I* get arrested. So she basically got to go live with her dad. And now she's suffering from that because she had her own room and everything at my house and she doesn't have that now.

My daughter's world would be lost without me, seriously. You know, kids today are so different than when I was growing up. Now they have *rights*.

It sounds like your daughter thought the grass would be greener, but is realizing she had it pretty good before.

A: Right, exactly.

Is there anything when you were a kid that was better or worse compared to now when it comes to our country or its politics?

A: I think things are a lot worse now. Parents are scared to let their kids out of their sight because of all the violence. If I had an African-American son, I would never want him to be out by himself, like I would literally pick him up, drop him off, or have someone pick him up and drop him off, because, it's like, the world has gotten to the point where they're looking at the color of your skin.

And you didn't feel that was the case when you were growing up? Did you experience racism?

A: No, not at all. I don't think it was the case when I was growing up. My daughter danced in a stepping group. They did a show for Black History Month. They were going through all the names of black people killed by the police...Trayvon Martin...it was then that I realized that my daughter knew more about Trayvon Martin than I did. I didn't think about that at her age. I sit down at night with her and we have conversations about it.

It's interesting to hear you say that you think police relations with the black community were actually better when you were growing up, that you feel less safe now.

A: I know these African American people have gotten killed for no reason.

When you were growing up did your parents talk about these same issues that you talk about with your daughter?

A: No. I'm realizing it more and more, how things were better for me as a child. You know, there was kinda no color line. I grew up with friends from a lot of different nationalities, but my black friends now will say, "How can you be friends with so and so?" because he or she is white.

I'm like, "We grew up together...I know they're not going to try and shoot me."

What do you think about the status of America? Where can we improve?

A: I think the United States, once it gets back on its feet...

JS: Alice quickly associated America's report card with its leader.

A: But you know, I'm not a Trump supporter. Never have, never will be. Everybody else wears a face mask but him. (Alice laughs.)

What don't you like about him?

A: It's just like, the things that he says...Oh my, he made a comment the other day, something about black people being called colored. And I'm like, "I thought the only thing you colored was on a piece of paper."

There are so many things that pop up on my phone every day about the things he says. I know right now, I know a lot of my people are upset because Trump planned a rally for Juneteenth. I'm like, "What do *you* know about Juneteenth?"

Did you like Bernie Sanders or any of the 2020 candidates who are out of the race now?

A: I did...I didn't vote for Hillary in 2016 though. I just didn't think that the country was ready for a woman president.

Will you vote for Biden?

A: Yes, I will.

Do you like him?

A: I do. I like his views and I like how he says things. You know, I think that you can probably talk to him and he would actually listen to you and take it in consideration versus Trump who'll probably tell you to go somewhere.

Have you participated in any of the rallies or the protests?

A: Oh no, no.

But you believe in what they're protesting?

A: If it's civil.

What are your thoughts on when Black Lives Matter protests are not civil? Do you see it as people at a breaking point?

A: Yeah but they're doing it in all the wrong ways. They're destroying communities. People have worked very hard to get these small businesses and you guys are just going and tearing them up. What's that solving? You're not going to bring the man back. I just think that it's totally uncalled for.

Do you feel like society at large doesn't understand what it's like to be black in America today?

A: I don't think they really understand because slavery goes back four-hundred years. I didn't necessarily know about Childish Gambino before, but a lot of kids know about him. I had to watch his video *This is America* over and over so I could catch everything and I'm like, wow.

JS: Childish Gambino is the stage name for American rapper Donald Glover. His 2018 song *This is America* is a brutal commentary on gun violence in America, specifically how it affects black Americans at a disproportionate rate.

What did you think about the video?

A: I just thought it was really, really bad, really awful, especially the part where they went inside a church and shot up people.

JS: This section of the video is likely referencing the Charleston, South Carolina church shooting which occurred on June 17, 2015. A white man shot and murdered nine congregants during a Bible study at the Emanuel African Methodist Episcopal Church.

A: There's a lot of really bad stuff in that video against black people. I have never, and maybe I've missed something, but I've never seen a white person hung. That is never shown. Still, it's not going to change how I feel about my Caucasian friends because I have a lot of them. I have a lot of nationalities in my friends.

Do you think it would have been challenging if you hadn't gone to a diverse high school?

A: I think so.

What are your greatest wishes for the world, for your daughter?

A: I just want everybody to get along, which I know is not going to happen.

What do we need to do to make that happen?

A: Come together as one, like no color lines.

How do we do it? Where does it start?

A: I think it starts in the home.

Chapter 5

"A New Democrat"
Brendan

"Community Minded"
Christian

Brendan
"A New Democrat"

Born—1998 in Denver, Colorado
Political Identity—Socially Liberal,
Fiscally Conservative

After Brendan's parents divorced when he was seven years old, he lived primarily with his mother. When Brendan was a junior in high school he lived with his father in Minnesota for the school year, a time Brendan recalls when he first started to pay attention to the nation's political landscape.

Brendan watched the 2016 presidential debates with his father because Brendan knew it would be the first election in which he would be old enough to vote. The match-up between Hillary Clinton and Donald Trump would make history either way, which was not lost on Brendan. He noted the significance of his first vote, between the first woman to run for president on a major party ticket and a businessman, someone who had never held political office.

Since 2016 Brendan has continued to pay attention. During our conversation Brendan came across as thoughtful, humble, honest, and refreshing. He claims to be socially liberal and fiscally conservative, but when pressed, that is more an aspiration, modeling himself after the example his mother has shown. We talked about what Brendan sees for his future and how things like climate change and stricter gun control might change that future.

Many times, Brendan tied his beliefs back to 2020 presidential candidate and Democratic hopeful Andrew Yang, of whom Brendan is a loyal supporter. Simply put, Brendan equated Yang with common sense. Whether we talked about a trickle-up economy or universal healthcare, Brendan felt aligned with Yang's policy stances.

Brendan also talked about jobs, the economy, and what it's like to be a white male living in the twenty-first century. Recently diagnosed with leukemia, Brendan has been given a close-up view of healthcare in America and he had opinions about that too.

What is your earliest memory of being shaped politically?

B: I don't remember a catalyst moment, but I grew up with President Obama. I was a fan.

My mother is socially liberal and fiscally conservative. My dad is very political; he's very liberal.

When I lived with him he would play the news, mainly MSNBC and Rachel Maddow, while he worked. We'd watch the Trump and Hillary debates…It was nice feeling that I was current on things because of my dad. He was an inspiration to me that way.

What did you think of Hilary Clinton and Donald Trump while they were campaigning?

B: I thought Donald Trump was flamboyant and privileged. I never grew up with Trump; I never watched his show (The Apprentice). I wasn't a big fan of Hillary's either. I voted for her because I didn't want to split the party. I was more for Bernie (Sanders).

Are you for Bernie in 2020?

JS: This conversation took place in late summer, 2019, before Bernie Sanders saw a surge in the polls.

B: For 2020 I am for Andrew Yang. I think he has accomplished a lot already. I don't know how far Bernie will go this time. I think he may be past his time. Part of it could be identity politics…Bernie is another old, white guy in office.

You mentioned "white guy" as though that is a bad thing, but you are a white male. How is it for you, being a white male in America in 2019?

B: I feel guilty and privileged. I want to give back to communities somehow. I've looked into working for FEMA (Federal Emergency Management Agency). That is something that is on my mind a lot.

Why do you feel guilty? Did you do something wrong or do you feel judged for being a white male?

B: I take more offense to the "man" part than I do the "white" part. It's mainly that I think white people, as a culture, have been kind of crappy to others over the past few hundred years or more.

To me, I think that when things get tough, white communities tend to blame others and throw shade and just not be constructive. I think communities of color, African American communities, come together a lot better and keep their heads strong.

Tell me more about your excitement about Andrew Yang's candidacy.

B: Andrew has these big ideas, but when he talks about them, he backs them up with facts and numbers. He sounds like he knows what he's talking about more than anybody else does. He doesn't badmouth anybody, and he will always answer a question straight up.

How did you become a fan?

B: I started watching some of his videos. He stood out with new ideas. He's a Democrat, but he's in favor of smaller government. Compared to him, the rest of the (2020) competitors seem old and stale.

Why do you say you're fiscally conservative?

B: There are a lot of people who are good with money-I'm not but I'd like to be. Andrew Yang says most people are socially liberal and fiscally conservative. I think that sounds about right. My mom has always been fiscally conservative too.

JS: Brendan lives outside of Dallas, Texas. In June, 2018 he was diagnosed with Acute Lymphoblastic Leukemia and had to take a break from college during treatment. He plans to return to college once he's no longer required to take immuno-suppressant pills. This medication is very common for transplant patients and helps prevent Graft vs. Host Disease (GVHD).

How has your illness impacted your political story? Has it given you time to think about medical care?

B: I've had a lot of time to think. My nurse practitioners and doctors have spent hours arguing with the insurance companies...I mean it just doesn't stop. In the end, we get what we need. We always get it; the insurance companies just put us through the ringer first.

Andrew Yang supports a public healthcare system. He doesn't want to take away private healthcare, he just wants to bring prices down and have some private competition in the field, which I think would be helpful.

What issues are most important to you right now?

B: Jobs and the economy. Yang talks about A.I. (artificial in-telligence) taking over the job market and how it's already happened to four million manufacturing jobs in most of the swing states that it took to get Trump elected.

Universal Basic Income would be a big help to the wage gap in this country and it would also help with racial inequality disparities. It would go to everybody. Yang calls this the trickle-up economy and not the trickle-down economy, which we know doesn't work. I believe in the trickle-up economy.

Young people are leading the charge on climate change. Is that a high priority for you?

B: Definitely. The Amazon is burning; farmers are burning fields under the direction of their president. The Amazon is the lungs of the Earth.

JS: Though surprising to hear, Brendan, like many other young people his age, believe that the Earth is nearing its end.

B: Some say the Earth will be uninhabitable in two years. I think it'll be more like ten or twelve years. Yang wants to do a lot for climate change, but he does say that there are going to be some effects we won't be able to change because they are already in swing, like flooding and wildfires. I definitely worry about it and I question having kids because of it, but I still have hope.

What else are you hopeful for?

B: Whether Andrew Yang is elected; I hope he is. In the coming years, in the A.I. age, I think trade jobs will last a lot longer, jobs in painting, carpentry, and building things will be emphasized. I want to go into tech theater—that's the building of sets and props and costumes. I did that in Minnesota.

I want to know your thoughts on a few issues, starting with guns and gun legislation.

141

B: I think there definitely needs to be gun control, but I don't think militarization is the way to go. I think (2020 Democratic Presidential candidate) Beto (O'Rourke) lost support when he went out and said, "Hell yeah, we'll take your assault rifles and AR-15s."

There's a new technology where a gun can read a person's hand grip. Andrew Yang wants to switch out a bunch of guns for people to trade them for the specific grip. But overall, we obviously have a problem in this country with gun violence. I don't see why background checks and mental health screenings are such a big deal.

What would be a good way to handle immigration? What do you think about "the wall" that President Trump campaigned on in 2016?

B: Back to Andrew Yang. Andrew talks about how Trump can get the problems right sometimes, but he has no idea how to make a solution. Trump blames immigrants for people losing their jobs in America, but Andrew blames A.I. I think that is more reasonable. I mean, this country was built on immigrants. We're all descendants of immigrants. The wall is not going to last...

How is it being a Democrat living in a red state?

B: In Texas, most of the big cities, maybe all of them, are blue, and the smaller towns around them, everywhere else, are red. I think where I live is more blue. My high school also had three thousand people in it. There's a good liberal population where I live and I feel like a lot of people are feeling kind of the same way as I am.

Do you pay attention to local politics too?

B: Not really, but I do think local politics can be as important as presidential elections. For instance, the Electoral College runs things in a way. How we vote locally for our members of Congress and for our senators can reshape the Electoral College.

What gives you hope for the future? Where do you think the United States is doing things right?

B: I think social media opens a lot of doors, and things like YouTube, new forms of public news or whatever. I think that we need to get the media under control though. When they started running twenty-four hour news channels for shock value, the media kind of got out of control with ratings. I don't think you can trust mainstream media now. I've heard it called the fourth branch of government. They're all very biased.

JS: We talked more about how Brendan researches for facts from many different media in order to draw his own conclusions.

B: I'm not a fan of Fox News. Except for when Andrew Yang is on there; he gets everyone's attention.

People are also reading less, so it's harder to get a full story.

B: Yes, we just get a headline to form an opinion. I try to go beyond that. I'm always finding podcasts or YouTube videos to get more information.

Much of our conversation led back to Andrew Yang. Your passion for his candidacy is really interesting.

B: Yeah, the Yang Gang is really passionate and vocal.

Would you ever consider campaigning for him?

B: Yeah, I think that would be fun. Once I get off immuno-suppressant pills I'll be able to go out more.

It sounds like even besides his policies you mostly like who Andrew Yang is as a person; you like his character.

B: Yeah. He seems like a self-made American. He really seems to care about everybody. He talks about how stay-at-home moms' work at home raising children is valued at zero, and we know that's not the case. I really like that Andrew wants our country to invest more in children; he sees children as an investment.

Brendan and His Dad

Christian
"Community Minded"

Born—1994 in Louisville, Kentucky
Political Identity—Conservative

When Christian was six years old his mother and father moved Christian and his younger twin brothers from Kentucky to just outside of Nashville, Tennessee. Christian has lived in that area ever since and as a young man his love for his community remains deep.

Christian comes across as a natural leader with an optimistic outlook on life, qualities that are reflected in his politics. He identifies as a conservative primarily from a belief that the federal government should have a limited role in people's lives. Christian believes any perceived gaps should not be filled by more government, but by neighbors helping neighbors.

Time and again, themes surrounding community, self-reliance, and small government came up during my interview with Christian. He pays attention to local and federal issues and frequently told personal anecdotes which show how his political beliefs have crystalized through the years, ranging from an epiphany he had as a high school student in the aftermath of a historic flood hitting Nashville, his takeaways after a fifty-pound weight loss, and, surprisingly, that even though Christian is a millennial, he is the first one to tell people to put their phones away and talk face-to-face instead.

Like Brendan (A New Democrat), Christian represents a slice of our country's future. He shared what his American Dream looks like, what he thinks about climate change, and what it was like growing up amid the white noise of school shootings, an omnipresent, somewhat desensitized, part of his reality.

When did you first become interested in politics or feel your own convictions starting to form?

C: I started getting interested in politics in late high school. I started doing my own research into different issues. It was a build up over time until then.

I always saw my dad as proof that as long as you work your tail off and do what you're supposed to do and do it right, you can live a successful and a happy life. He taught my brothers and me that you're not going to be a super-star all of the time, but as long as you're making a living, and you're able to provide for your family, and love your family, and do all that, then life's good.

Would he say that to you consciously or model it?

C: More the model, but I do remember him saying it too, especially once I got my first job and started bringing in money. I remember if I said, "Uh, I don't want to go to work today...I'm going to call in."

My dad would say, "No, we don't call out in this household. We don't do that here."

A lot of things I am glad he said now. The main way I look at things now is that there are no handouts. You have to earn everything you get. Anything I do I have to earn it.

JS: Christian tied his view on self-reliance to a story about his recent weight loss.

C: I went from two hundred twenty-five to one hundred seventy pounds and I had to earn that. I'm the reason I got to two hundred twenty-five in the first place. I put myself in a bad place because I was putting junk food in my body non-stop and I was putting sugar and carbs that I didn't need in my body

148

every day. The only way to be successful is through yourself. I had to force myself to better myself.

How does that view blend with your conservative ideology?

C: The more the government wants to help you, especially big government, the messier things get. I think local government can be more involved, because they're more hands-on with what's going on.

JS: Christian tied this thinking to his memory of when downtown Nashville was flooded in 2010 while he was still in high school.

C: Water got in the Grand Ole Opry and the Rhinehart Auditorium, but we really didn't get any federal help. It was 2010, so the economy wasn't great, but our local politicians said, "Hey, we're going to overcome this."

On the same day the flood happened, there was an oil spill in the Gulf. I remember thinking, "We're stuck in this historic flood and on every news channel the only thing I'm seeing is about the oil spill."

I thought, "Man, no one cares about Nashville nationally."

But as a community we were joining together. We were going out to schools that were completely ruined and gutted, and cleaning out these small little creeks for weeks at a time.

I think that was a big start for me. I realized that instead of focusing on the federal government we should be focused more on our local government. We need to rely on the few people we elect locally instead of the people who were elected to help hundreds of millions of Americans.

That was a big moment for me when I look back at it.

JS: It was about the same time when Christian noticed what he perceived as media bias, in this case pushing a narrative that Christian knew to be untrue.

C: All the time I wonder why one thing gets covered in the news versus some other thing. And then we also see certain agendas being pushed.

We had a student here in Nashville who went into a Waffle House and shot it up. There were people I went to high school with who were shot by him and some were killed. I remember seeing it. I worked right down the road and remember seeing someone being carried out by the coroner. I was like, "What the hell is happening?"

It turns out it was a crazed man, but thankfully a local hero went in and grabbed the gun from the guy. The shooter stripped down naked and ran off and hid in the woods for two days.

The shooter was white and several of the victims were black. I watched it later on the news and saw they'd turned it into a race thing. I was like, "This is far from a race thing down here."

This is one of the most diverse areas in Nashville. We have a good amount of white people, black, Hispanic, a lot of Kurdish people…It's a very diverse community, but they're trying to make it look like our community is racist.

Now, it was a crazy man. He was messed up, on some type of drug, and went crazy. I don't think race was a motive. I thought, "Why are we creating this divide?"

Are there local or national candidates who you like? Do you always vote Republican?

C: The last presidential election was the first one I voted in. I voted for Governor Gary Johnson because he didn't seem crazy. That's my go-to with my gut.

JS: Gary Johnson ran as a Libertarian for President of the United States in both the 2012 and 2016 elections.

C: I would like to vote for a Democrat but I haven't, mainly because the party seems to be going further and further to the left, with socialist agendas like Elizabeth Warren's and Bernie Sanders'. It goes back to what I've been saying - small government is what needs to be focused on.

When you give it up to the federal government it's more red tape, more red tape, which means more problems. When the government says, "We're going to fix this problem," another problem pops up, and it just becomes a knotted spider web of issues. Our government will ultimately crumble because it can't handle all of the issues.

What role should the federal government take, in your opinion?

C: Let federal government handle foreign policy and major issues that affect multiple states.

For example, Texas and Tennessee have done a good job of growing. Even with the flooding, Nashville has kept on trucking. So instead of (politicians) shouting, "I've got an idea...I've got an idea!" big government should look at these cities and states that are successful and say, "How can we adopt that? How can other states adopt that?"

I think the federal government should also step in when it comes to immigration. That's all so messed up. It's become one of those balls of web. I say let's start over and work with Mexico and other countries as well. Obviously, we can't put all the focus on our southern border. We can't disregard people coming in from Asia, Europe, and Canada.

We have to be fair to everyone who wants to better their lives and come to America. Ultimately isn't that the reason

151

ninety-nine percent of people are coming here, for a better life and better opportunities? We need to press reset and make a clear immigration process. It might take a little bit of time, but we need to go through it. I've read reports that a main issue right now is expired visas. A lot of people are not updating the government and/or are missing their court dates.

JS: Christian tied his stance on immigration to another personal story.

C: One of my best friend's dad came here from Mexico. It was a long process, but he did it right. He went to every court date, and proved he had a source of income and had somewhere to live. As long as he kept proving that and made his court dates, they kept telling him to keep doing his thing.

He became an American citizen. He went back to Mexico, got his wife, and they had kids in the United States. He has passed away now, but he was a good father and a good role model to my friend.

JS: What Brendan (A New Democrat) had to say about being a white male in America today made me think about what Christian's white *conservative* experience has been like.

What has your experience been like being a young, white, conservative male in America today?

C: The hardest thing about being a male is approaching fe-males. Man, you get shut down so fast. I try to be nice. I'll say, "Hi, I'm Christian. Could I get your phone number or your Instragram?"

They take offense and act like I'm doing something to them. Or when I'm trying to get to know a girl, as soon as they see my Instragram, or one bit of my political beliefs, they try to shut me off.

I'm like, "Why?"

I am glad to know early on that's how they are though, because it wouldn't work out between us anyway. If they're that shallow, it's not going to work.

Also, being a white male, I work collections and have a wide customer base. I get called racist fairly often. I know it's in anger because no one wants me collecting from them. But it's offensive to be compared to the lowest, lowest people of the earth just because I'm white.

I want to say, "You don't even know me like that." When people have called me "racist" it's just a low blow, beneath the belt. I've gotten used to it though, and I don't get as pissed as I used to get.

How do you not take it personally?

C: I hate to say it, but if I'm going back and forth with whoever and they throw that racist line, I know I won that argument. I know they don't have a valid comeback when they say that. It's just a conversation ender because they don't have anything else to say.

You're a millennial and somewhat old fashioned. Do you open doors for others?

C: I hold the door for everybody. Opening doors is something my parents taught me and my brothers. Growing up I remember wanting to get out of church so fast, but when we'd start to rush for the doors my dad said, "Hold the door open."

Before I knew it, we held the door open for all 200 people in the church. We would hate it but now I do it every day; it's a natural thing. You still see a lot of that down here in the South. When you're walking down the street there's a lot of eye contact and, "Hey, how you doing?"

There's a sense of community in the South. I noticed when I go outside it I don't see that same sense of community, not as much "help thy neighbor," if you know what I mean.

How is it living in a red state? Do you know any difference?

C: Where I live, Nashville, is pretty blue. Once you go outside to these little towns, there's even more a sense of community and they vote more red, more Republican, because they're still relying on their local government to take care of them.

They know whoever the president is for four or eight years doesn't care about John in Smithsville, Tennessee, or about anyone at the Tyson plant in Shelbyville, or the farmer in Murfreesboro. I think that's one of the reasons we see that in small towns there's still a heavy reliance on local government.

From your point of view, do you feel like life in America is better now or when your grandparents were young?

C: Definitely life is better now than it was then but there were some benefits growing up then. Again, there was more community.

I feel lucky to have grown up in the '90s and early 2000s because I actually played with toys instead of watching kids play with toys or watching my friends watch YouTube videos. Our house was the house with all the bikes out front. We had a group of guys who met up every day after school and we'd play touch football or go to the field. One summer we had our own Olympic Games.

I think kids today aren't as active and so they have more pent up energy, but that energy needs to be released. You feel good and more confident when you get a good workout or work up a sweat.

The ones that are addicted to being on their phones and sit there and are always watching YouTube videos and don't socialize really, those are the kids that worry me. Those are the ones that are going to have health issues; those are the ones who will not be able to communicate and live in society.

You see people my age who are like that. You're shopping at the grocery store and their heads are down in their phone while they shop. I don't know how that's possible. I'm only looking to see if I got stuff on my list. I'm looking at the shelves for the best deals.

What do you think is better about living today?

C: For one thing, I think that in the next seventy years, hopefully in my lifetime, we'll be able to read people's minds. I think technology will get there.

Young people are on the forefront of climate change and many have expressed doubt that the world will even exist that long. The United States is the second largest polluter after China. What do you think? Are you hopeful for the future?

C: I think climate change is real. My thing is, why is it just an American issue? It is a global issue. If we want to affect change, we have to say, "Hey, get it together," to other countries. "If you want our products, if you want to do trade with us, then stop using all these oils and coal."

We could step in to help them be greener and healthier. We're already starting to see small changes in the ecosystem and in the environment. We can't say, "Here's the solution—we're going to do it right now."

We need to have all the answers. I want to know who the top five percent experts in the world are on this. Get them together and say, "This is your job. Figure out what we have to do." Pay them big money to do it.

The whole world needs to fix it though, not just us. I think in the long run we are going to get there.

Are there areas where you think America could be doing better?

C: There are always areas to do better in anything we do. No one's perfect. We keep trying to get better and better. The iPhone was cool and all, but the iPhone 11 is even better. You can always point fingers. Instead be the model example. The United States is the best at anything we put our minds to, and I think we can be with climate change issues too. I hope we keep raising the bar and getting better.

JS: Like Brendan, it was interesting to hear a young person's views on politics and we often went off topic a bit to discuss American culture at large. Christian's view of the world through a community-minded lens (or lack thereof) reminded me that many problems stem back to people not sitting together in person and talking like neighbors.

Smart phone technology came out when you were in middle school. A lot of kids today don't remember a time without it. Do you remember what it was like without a smart phone?

C: The Motorola RAZR was the best phone in middle school.

JS: Christian laughed at the memory and tied early phones to simpler times in his life.

C: I go back to approaching girls again. They're not used to being approached by guys and guys aren't used to approaching girls. They're used to swiping right and hoping to get a match.

You still hope for the best. You might fail, but you're hoping for that one time. Who knows? You might find the love of your life.

Do you believe that access to smartphones has impacted and changed people's social skills?

C: Absolutely. I think it will better itself, but I don't have a solution. It might be easier if we could read each other's minds. I think, I am hoping, we will have the technology to do that in my lifetime.

JS: Christian laughed half-heartedly, before growing earnest again.

C: I think everyone should take a thirty-day break at least once a year from social media. It frees up your mind. It makes you look at the world differently. I promise that. I do it every so often and by about a week in, I realize I'm more focused on my job, my health, and more focused on other things that are better for me.

One of my favorite games to play at family reunions is to say, "Hey, put your phone on the table. The first one whose phone goes off loses."

I've done that because I would get mad at some of my cousins. We'd be sitting around at a table and the first night we're together they're tossing around their phones, either texting their girlfriend or boyfriend or scrolling mindlessly. I'm like, "Hey put your phones down and let's go!"

I even do it when I sit down to eat with my brothers and parents. Three out of five have their phone out. I'm like, "Put your phone in the middle of the table!"

Where do you think that comes from? Does it tie back to your love of community?

C: Thankfully the Joe Rogan podcast. A lot of people my age look up to Joe Rogan. He thinks a lot about the way our world and our country should be viewed. He says not to blindly pick a side, but look at every side of an issue, and then make your opinion or find a solution. Usually the solution is somewhere down the middle with two people yelling at each other.

In one podcast (Rogan) said, "You don't know how many people can't sit for one-and-a-half to three hours and not glance at their phone."

I realized he was right. If you can't sit and talk to someone for an hour-and-a-half without looking at your phone...Joe Rogan says, "First off, it's so disrespectful to the person you're talking to. Second, it proves you have an issue. You're addicted to that screen."

I'm glad I was born in the mid-90s because I feel like I'm from the last generation that didn't have constant connectivity to the world. I can only imagine how it would be like if on 9/11 everyone had phones. Not just the recording that would have gone down, but can you imagine the videos that would have come out from inside the World Trade Center?

There is so much more stuff now, which is good and bad. We need to use the best of it to our advantage and remember with all this technology and all this good, there is some bad that comes with it. We need to fix the bad ourselves. We need to own up to it.

JS: Again, because he is so much younger, I found Christian's views as refreshing as interviewing older subjects, both reflective of unique times living in America.

What was it like growing up with school shootings in America becoming a regular occurrence?

C: I was thinking about that the other day. I heard a news report about kids being prepped for a school shooter. I remember being in first grade and going in our little bathroom in our teacher's class and her closing the blinds and putting a door stop in the door for an active shooter.

Was that scary to you?

C: I remember thinking it was weird. I was a first grader and I'm in a small, little bathroom with twenty-five little classmates and my teacher. To me it went along with the tornado test and the fire drills. Be prepared for anything. Practicing that stuff, thinking about that stuff, I'd rather be prepared if anything happens. If someone were to come and shoot up the shopping center where I work, it's good to know where I'm going to go.

Are there any issues that worry you or that threaten your vision of the American Dream?

C: I worry if we don't fight socialism now, that by the time I'm seventy years old America will be a dump. Socialism works on a small scale. If you have a group of your friends, your own little community, and you had the right resources to eat, sleep, and live, it works. But when you get to something as large scale as our country is with fifty states, it always seems to fail.

You say "socialism," but what area in your life would be affected most?

C: Healthcare would be first. We already have long wait times. The sense is if you rely on government to take care of it, next thing you know we'll be hearing, "We don't think you're too bad right now…you're on a waiting list for treatment."

I remember reading that if you couldn't pay for a surgery in the 1960s, 1970s, or in the 1980s that doctors would do elective surgery for preventive care and take care of it, or charity would help pay for it. It's back to the small community aspect. Now there's government interference and the prices to the consumer have skyrocketed. I get government regulations, but the more they get involved, the more red tape there is, and then the higher the product cost.

How should we pay for people who can't afford health insurance?

C: For those who can't afford it, that's where that sense of smaller community needs to step in, or at least I hope it would. Instead of relying on government to be something for you, there are people who are willing to help you.

I remember an older man who always stood in front of a courthouse, talking to everybody. He didn't have health insurance but needed a surgery, so the people of Lebanon, Tennessee chipped in and helped him out. They took care of what he needed.

It's easier now to raise money this way, like with Go Fund Me. It's not just in your community now either; people are willing to chip in from all over the world. There's a guy who made a million dollars saying, "Hey, I need beer on college game day."

Then he donated it to a children's hospital…that guy's great.

What do you think is the answer when it comes to gun legislation, especially because the solutions from both sides are so disparate?

C: If you go to two polar ends the answer is going to be in the middle. We have the second amendment so that the federal government can't outweigh the people. We have our guns; we have some way to fight back if we mess up and elect the worst kind of people possible. You never know. That's my biggest argument on guns. We need them for the very worst-case scenario if we can't rely on our government to take care of us. I would rather gun legislation be left to the states because different states have different issues. For example, in Tennessee there is a lot of hunting.

Do you own a gun?

C: I don't own a gun, but I will probably own one eventually when I buy a house. There's always going to be guns on the street, but I'd rather have more good guys with guns than bad guys with guns. If we outlaw guns completely bad people are still going to figure out bad ways to hurt people. That will always be. I want good people to have the ability to defend themselves.

If we don't have the second amendment, we don't have anything.

I go back to thinking we should look to other states that are doing things well, or not so well. Like why are there strict gun policies in Illinois, but Chicago has so many shootings?

Do you support the Trump administration?

C: I can't complain. When he got elected, I said, "He isn't Gary Johnson, but he's our president."

Policy-wise President Trump has been okay. My life is better now than before he was elected. I'm making more money; I've invested in stocks. As long as the economy keeps riding like it's been, I have nothing against him. It would be good to hear from him on Twitter once a week at the most, though.

Would you ever vote for a Democrat?

C: I would love for a Democrat to win me over. I'm all for Tulsi Gabbard (a politician from Hawaii who as of press time was still in the field of Democratic contenders for president). I like her foreign policy, how she believes we need to focus on our own country. She has more of an isolationist policy, a "get out of these quasi-wars" and "let's free up that budget" view. She's someone you can have a conversation with; she's real. I also respect that she served in the military.

What is one way you wish citizens could take part in the political process?

C: I wish the American people had the ability to vote where they want their tax dollars spent. I'd like it if we could fill out an application when we're filling out our taxes and could check what percentage of our taxes we'd like to see go to each part of the budget. Then you can see where the American people really want to spend their money. Do they want to put more money toward climate change? Defense? The school system? I guarantee it would really change things if we let the American people choose.

Where would you want to put your money?

C: Definitely education. I look to the future.

What does the American Dream mean to you?

C: For me, success is being around loved ones. I love being with family and I always have my arms open to friends. I don't hold a grudge and do what I can to help others. Helping others is a great feeling.

I see so many people strive and focus on their career, but to me a job is a job; it's forty to fifty hours a week. I like getting a little overtime every now and then, but outside of that it's just a job. I try to live my dream by living as healthy as possible and as happy as possible and hopefully someday soon I'll find the woman of my dreams. I'd like to own a home and have a family.

The American Dream to me is being able to do what you want and choose the path you want to go. You may have to work a little bit harder based on where you come from, and who you are, to get where you want to go, but if you put your heart and mind to it, it's possible. I look at professional athletes all the time and think about all the people that could have been a professional athlete, but they didn't put their heart and mind into it like these guys did.

There are so many obstacles, but there are so many people who came from poverty and have made it. The right people helped them out along the way; someone took them in…I think that's something I took from my mom. She has the biggest heart of anyone I know. She would give the shirt off her back to anyone who needed it.

Overall, I would say that I live by the belief that it's important to help others out…do unto others as you would have them do unto you.

Chapter 6

"The Humanist" Lily

"Defender of the Marginalized" Beatriz

Lily
"The Humanist"

Born—1947 in Detroit, Michigan
Political identity—Democrat

Lily's father was forty-five and her mother was thirty-seven when she was born—their "surprise" after having two older daughters. Lily may have been the baby of the family, but she was never coddled. She comes from a long line of no-nonsense, hard workers who were independent minded, something that played a prominent role in Lily's shaping. Her parents met years earlier while working on a railroad. Neither were high school graduates, but both made up for that with street smarts. When asked how her parents were influenced by World War II, Lily said they didn't talk about those years much, though she remembered that her mother "loved" President Franklin Delano Roosevelt (FDR).

"They talked more about the (Great) Depression and how that had eliminated opportunities for them and for others," Lily added. "My dad would often say, 'I wonder what I could have done.'"

Lily, like some of the other interviewees who were alive before the 1960s, pointed out that politics were not as partisan when she was young as they are today. By her memory, Lily said candidates seemed to be supported for their character traits and not their political party. Lily embraces this value when she is voting. She comes across as compassionate and loyal, and at the core of who she is, Lily values dignity and human rights over politics. Many of her priorities originate with women's rights, including access to birth control. She believes the 1973 Supreme Court decision of Roe vs. Wade has created a unique division in the United States.

While Lily is committed to being open-minded, which means open to candidates from both parties, she admitted she has grown more frustrated with Republican candidates and policies over the years, culminating with President Donald Trump's administration.

What did you see or hear as a child that added to your political shaping?

L: From a young age I had a connection to the Democrat Party because to me it was always the working man's party. Nobody from either my mother's or father's side were the "pillars of the community" types. They weren't professional or educated; they weren't homeowners, but they were hard workers. I've never been part of a union, but I wouldn't cross a picket line just because I think it's wrong. Maybe that was because of growing up in Detroit around the auto industry.

As I got older it used to blow my mind when someone I knew got an inheritance. I didn't resent it; it just seemed foreign to me because of my background.

Have you always voted for Democratic candidates?

L: No. It's interesting because the people I often admired and liked were Republican. They're the ones I used to love listening to. When I was growing up the issues weren't Democrat or Republican...they were just issues. I didn't really pay attention to what parties people were in either. There were pundits on TV, but people didn't talk about if they were Democrat or Republican. They didn't walk around with a label on their forehead like they do now.

Who are, or were, some of the politicians you have liked?

L: One of the Republicans I really liked was George H.W. Bush. He was a good man. In fact, I voted for him, and not Bill Clinton, in 1992.

JS: Lily talked for a bit about her positive feelings toward the elder President Bush, but those feelings didn't transfer to his son, the forty-third U.S. President, George W. Bush.

L: I saw him on television. He got up there and tried to talk like a good ol' boy, but he wasn't a good ol' boy. He was raised in extreme affluence, but there he was, talking like a cowboy. That turned me off.

Now I do think (George W. Bush) was a million times better than Donald Trump. Before Trump was in politics I had heard him years ago on the Howard Stern Show. I remember that he said horrible things about the women he was going out with, even though he was living at the time with Marla Maples. I remember him talking about other women and about their bodies. I couldn't believe it.

Are there also issues that make you align more with the Democratic Party?

L: Yes. Abortion is one area where I've evolved my thinking. I used to take a pro-life stance that was bred out of my Catholic faith and parochial school upbringing.

JS: Lily said the 1973 landmark Supreme Court decision in Roe vs. Wade, which ruled that a state law that banned abortions (except to save the life of the mother) was unconstitutional, was a game changer for her.

L: Up until a woman is three months pregnant it wasn't called an abortion years ago. When I was in high school and college, people used to have D&Cs frequently; they'd call it a "dusting and cleaning."

JS: Dilation and curettage (D&C) is an out-patient surgical procedure in which the cervix is dilated and an instrument is used to remove tissue from inside the uterus.

L: I realized later that getting a D&C was kind of a code word kind of thing (in some cases) for abortion and nobody cared. It was, "I have really bad cramps," or, "I have really heavy periods," so they would have a D&C.

I didn't know it then, but they were pregnant. I remember there were a couple of girls who just disappeared, and I learned later that they'd had children and that the babies were just taken as soon as they gave birth.

I don't agree that the exact second an egg is fertilized is the same as getting an abortion when you're five months pregnant. I worked with a woman who had several abortions. It was like her method of birth control and I thought it was gross. I'm sure there are people who do that, but there should be a different name for an early, early termination of a pregnancy. If it's early, it's nobody's business. It shouldn't be called an abortion.

Did you notice a change in society's views since Roe vs. Wade?

L: There has been a downside actually. It's been a cruel, very misogynistic, thing that's taken over the Right to Life Movement. Pro-choice versus pro-life positions have been an unfair fight.

JS: This discussion led Lily to broader points she feels strongly about regarding access to birth control and sex education.

L: If a woman (has an abortion) as a method of birth control she should be strongly encouraged to get sterilized if she doesn't want children, but birth control should be talked about; it should be explained and given out.

For some of those teenage mothers I learned about later, it could have been their first and only boyfriends. I'm not saying they should have had abortions. What they should have had was access to birth control. That infuriates me. It was humiliating for girls to request birth control back then.

JS: Lily called it a "complicated" as well as humiliating process, recalling her own experience when she sought contraception after being divorced with five children.

L: I went to the doctor to get a diaphragm. When he asked me if I might do something, I said, "I hope."
The doctor said, "You're kidding, right?"

JS: Lily left feeling humiliated, but this grew into a determination that her daughters and then granddaughters would never experience the same treatment.

L: I sent my kids to Planned Parenthood when they were in college. They could get medical care and birth control. It was important to me that they knew about it and it infuriates me that Planned Parenthood is demonized today.
Abortion is still sad and hurtful and may weigh on a woman forever, but that some believe women don't have that control over their bodies is misogynistic and primitive and I think one hundred years from now it will be recognized as such.

JS: When asked who she thinks holds the blame, Lily didn't pause. She puts the blame on politicians, explaining that they hold the most responsibility for making changes because they have the largest platforms. Instead, Lily believes politicians use religion as a scapegoat.

L: This puritanical, looney tunes stuff that the politicians do—they're using people's religious affiliations to take advantage of them.

You grew up in the Catholic Church. How did being raised Catholic shape your politics?

L: There are a lot of things about the Catholic Church I love, but they should have women with more senior roles in the church. It's ancient and primitive that they don't, and it pisses me off.

JS: Lily recalled her own years in the church, especially the kindergarten through twelfth grade Catholic education that she received.

L: We went to mass every day with school. I knew the entire mass in Latin, but I remember thinking that most of the boys didn't seem to care like I did. Yet I couldn't be an altar boy.

JS: Since the early 1980s both boys and girls have been allowed to be altar servers in Catholic parishes throughout the United States.

Did your parents revere church leaders?

L: I didn't have this "in awe" feeling about priests. I think my family had this thing where we questioned authority. My dad's father told him, "No man worth his salt goes to school past eighth grade" and I think my mother considered herself somewhat of a rebel too. She pitied priests more than she looked up to everything they had to say. I remember her saying, "Oh, look at what they have to wear," about priests to us.

JS: When she was a teenager Lily volunteered at a Catholic orphanage, the memory of which brought the conversation back to her thoughts on women's rights.

L: The orphanage was this gymnasium-size room filled with baby cribs and incubators as far as the eye could see. I can see it in my nightmares. The babies of girls who'd go away to Aunt Bertha's or somewhere really left school because they'd had these babies. Some of the babies were also there because their mothers were ill.

We'd take the children to the zoo…we'd play with them; they'd climb all over us and want to call us mama. Oh my god…it's seared in my memory.

If fathers couldn't care for their children because the mothers were sick or dead, these lovely, beautiful Sisters of Charity, who were like angels, took care of these children and the fathers would get them on weekends. The Sisters of Charity were true saints.

JS: At about the same time, Lily said she heard news about childcare centers in China, which were likened to these orphanages.

L: The way they were presented, it was like, "Oh my God, how awful." Well, I realized later, when daycare centers became common, that what they were showing us, those videos from China, were daycare centers.

What other issues make you believe that the Democratic Party is the right party for you?

L: I think that the whole notion behind "the wall" is stupid.

JS: President Donald Trump campaigned largely on a promise that he would build a barrier, or a wall, to stop people from entering the United States illegally through the southern border.

L: They're going to take people's lands to make a wall happen. You have to remember, Donald Trump is a reality TV star. He wanted his own TV show. He didn't think he was going to win.

There's this whole thing in this country, like with the college admissions scandal, that if you think you can get away with it, you should do it. It makes me want to vomit.

JS: In 2019 several wealthy celebrities were accused of paying large sums of money to universities, in exchange for admitting their children.

Do you think this is a political party characteristic?

L: I do think this thinking is much more prevalent with the people in the Republican party. They're using people's religions to say, "You can't do this," or, "You can't do that." A lot of times it is anti-gay, like not supporting transgender people in the military. What makes me mad is that this one characteristic is not the whole person. That is not their soul. Their sexuality is just one part of them. I don't get it and it has caused so much hatred. These attitudes used to be something that people kept to themselves, but they've become okay to express.

I am super in favor of the attitude of, "Why do we even have to mention it?" It's like, what color was your hair when you were born? It's just stupid. There's a lot of anti-accepting today. I don't get how you can condemn someone because of their sexual orientation or their skin color. I just don't get it.

When have you been proud of what is going on in the United States?

L: There was excitement the day after Obama was elected. Everyone was smiling at each other. There was an aura of good news. I really hope we can get back to that again.

Beatriz

"Defender of the Marginalized"

Born—1965 in Juarez, Mexico
Political Identity—Progressive

Beatriz never knew her biological father because he died before she was born. When her mother met and married a man who was half-Mexican, and an American citizen, Beatriz was five years old. She and her mother moved from Juarez, Mexico to El Paso, Texas to start a new life, but her heart never forgot her native Mexico. Beatriz and her mother went back to visit at least every summer. It was on one such trip that Beatriz noticed a camp of homeless people, the memory of which serves as a symbol for her political beliefs as a voice for the poor.

Throughout our conversation, Beatriz repeatedly brought up a stereotype that infuriates her—that Democrats want hand-outs. As she grew up Beatriz's experiences confirmed her beliefs time and again, but she was galvanized to take action in 2016 when then candidate Donald Trump campaigned on a promise to build a border wall. Beatriz thought that the language Trump used was so dehumanizing that she still gets upset when she talks about it. Since 2016 Beatriz has taken steps to make a difference. She has joined activist groups in her area and volunteers for several political campaigns, all with the hope that a progressive candidate will take the White House in 2020.

Like Lin (Goldilocks), Beatriz was inspired to become a U.S. citizen after watching the historically close presidential election in 2000. Coincidentally, Beatriz became an American citizen two days after 9/11, on September 13, 2001.

Beatriz has had many personal experiences which have shaped her politically. Like Teri and Lin, Beatriz described the omnipresent feeling of being a stranger in a strange land, starting with assimilation when she came to the United States as a young girl. Once a teenage mother, Beatriz also had a lot to say about women's rights. Her experience was nearly fifteen years after Lily's (The Humanist) memory of seeing unwed, pregnant teenagers swept from sight, but Beatriz touched on the same feelings of shame and isolation, which she turned into a challenge to not be a statistic, but to thrive.

More challenge would follow Beatriz. Despite living a healthy lifestyle, she was diagnosed with Chronic Myelogenous Leukemia when she was forty-five years old, which strengthened her resolve to also be an advocate for affordable healthcare.

What is your earliest memory of politics?

B: My mom was always very outspoken about the politics in Mexico. Growing up we talked about the political corruption there. I remember that when I came over to the United States, I wasn't allowed to enroll in school because I didn't speak English and then once I was allowed to go to school I wasn't allowed to go by the name I went by in Mexico. My family always called me "Bety" (Be-tee). On my first day, my teacher said, "No, that is the nickname for Elizabeth. So you need to think of a different nickname."

I had been working so hard to learn English to go to school, all I wanted to do was fit in. I felt alienated instead. I did a little bit of reading and saw that Bea is short for (the English spelling) Beatrice, so that's what I was called. My family still calls me "Bety," though.

JS: Beatriz's mother gave birth to another daughter, a half-sister, but Beatriz noted that their six year age difference and their different upbringings shaped them to be politically different.

B: My younger sister is my opposite politically. She is ultra-Tea Party conservative.

Why do you think you two are so different?

B: I think it's because when I first came to the States, my stepfather identified very much as a Democrat. He had even worked on Robert Kennedy's presidential campaign. And then when I was about ten my stepfather started changing into a conservative. He had read some stuff about corruption in the Chicago elections and I think that really turned him off. My sister was about five by then, so the rest of her upbringing she was brought up conservative.

179

Did your stepfather remain just as passionate about politics, only for a different party?

B: Oh, yeah. In fact, he has donated a lot of money to the Trump campaign. So much so that Trump sent him a personal letter to say thank you. It almost made me throw up.

JS: Beatriz's mother and stepfather went on to divorce when Beatriz was twelve.

Were you involved in politics as you grew up?

B: In high school I was really involved in student government. I read about Watergate and became familiar with Nixon. I guess, I don't want to say that people who aren't liberal aren't compassionate, I don't mean that at all. But I remember when we would drive from Mexico to El Paso and we would cross the same bridge. There were people begging for money in the hot sun with their babies in their arms. There were people who were disabled and in wheelchairs, just asking for any handouts we had. My mom never referred to them as people that didn't want to work. She had compassion and would always give them a little bit of money or some food. Those images still stick in my mind because I never thought of those people as bad or lazy.

They simply found themselves in circumstances that I felt we can be compassionate toward. It's crazy to me that there are people in countries that don't have a lot of resources and they're poor, and we're going to belittle them for their circumstances?

I think that's really what shapes my narrative, my own personal views. I don't like people being referred to as "lazy," and anyone who refers to Mexicans as "illegals…"

JS: At this point Beatriz choked back her emotion.

B: I think when Trump said, "Mexico isn't sending their best," I knew that was so untrue. I thought, "Oh my God." I came over here as a little girl and I've worked since I was fifteen years old. I used to ride my bike to get to work. Nobody gave me a couple of million dollars as a loan. I worked full-time so I could support my daughter and put myself through school. So having my whole people be called "lazy" or "not the best" to come to this country, I don't think I could ever forgive that.

Have you always identified with Democratic Party candidates?

B: Yes. I'm a yellow dog Democrat. I vote blue no matter who. If it's two Democrats running against each other, I usually identify with the more progressive candidate.

I decided not to put off becoming a citizen any longer after the 2000 election when Al Gore lost Florida. I thought, "Oh my god." There were such few votes that made the difference in that election, I realized I had to get my citizenship.

Was becoming a citizen daunting to you? Why did you wait after living in the United States for thirty years?

B: I've always been proud of my Mexican heritage. I never felt a big push to be an American citizen because I was a legal resident, but then Gore lost the election and I was just so angered by how that transpired, I filed my paperwork to become a citizen. I have voted in every election ever since, even the little ones, the local ones.

What is your vision for your personal American Dream or for the country? What would make the country ideal for you?

B: Healthcare is definitely a big concern, especially at my age. Even if I had the financial means to retire early or, God forbid, if I get laid off from my job, I don't have that peace of mind that I'll be okay because of how healthcare is in the U.S. Healthcare can be tied to working until you're sixty-five because, gosh, to be without health insurance is a death sentence. I've had cancer so I'm a high risk. Every time these politicians talk about the threat to the Affordable Care Act and not covering pre-existing conditions it affects me. And I am the picture of health if people could see me. I run, I eat right, I drink my one glass of wine the way doctors recommend. Even after all that, I still got cancer. What the hell are you supposed to do then?

How are you doing now? As a leukemia survivor, you probably have opinions on healthcare.

B: I'm doing great; I'm really lucky. I had a good paying job and great benefits so I was very fortunate to get the care I needed, but man, if I didn't have the insurance I had, it wouldn't have been good. They would have had to put me on a medication that was less expensive than the medication they put me on, and the cheaper medication, people would tell me that when they took it, a side effect was that their eyes would bleed. I'm just so lucky.

What other issues are priorities to you?

B: I want compassionate immigration reform, especially with Dreamers. They should have a chance to stay in the country and work. I'm also concerned about climate change, human rights, LGBTQ rights…

Regarding climate change, what do you think we should be doing right now?

B: No brainers would be cutting back on fossil fuels and making sure our cars are EPV (Environmental Performance Vehicles). The environment should be protected by not allowing companies to pollute our waterways and our air.

Abortion rights are also in my top five priorities. Now you can see why I'm Democrat, probably.

I had my daughter on my own. Having raised her as a single parent, and working my way through school, I think that has also shaped me. I always had to care for myself. Now I'm married and my daughter is grown. She is also married and luckily made it out.

I know I worked hard. I got pregnant in high school, so the chances of me even graduating from college were very low, but I graduated with a bachelor's degree and went on to get my MBA. I consider myself very fortunate.

Why do you think you beat the odds?

B: Maybe part of it was the challenge. In high school I had to go to a special program for pregnant girls. We couldn't be seen by the general school population because that would encourage the other girls to get pregnant, they said. That was the policy at the time. I remember the teacher talking about the big challenge ahead of us, and showing us the statistics, and I thought, "I'm not going to be a statistic. One of these days I want to get my master's degree."

I also worked at a grocery store and a lot of the people my age were college students and they really encouraged me to go to school and get a degree. I remember a friend from work going with me to register for college and really giving me that push. The challenge and the support were heavy influences.

JS: My conversation with Beatriz took place six weeks after a gunman shot and killed twenty-two people and injured twenty-four others inside the Walmart in El Paso, Texas.

You live near El Paso. How were you impacted by the shooting inside Walmart?

B: My mother goes to an elderly daycare and one of their regular activities is to go to that Walmart. She called me very upset; she was frightened because she heard that Mexicans had been targeted because that idiot wrote about it.

At first no one had the facts. They thought there were multiple shooters at first. My mom said, "What if they try to break into my house?" I tried to calm her down. She was so upset. My mom is really sweet.

This reminds me that I also believe in strong gun control. That's definitely in my top five of most important issues. Even though this country would never go for a gun buyback as some of the politicians have proposed, I am personally for that.

Are there any candidates you're excited about?

B: I hoped Beto O'Rourke would pull off a miracle and I love Elizabeth Warren. Really, whoever the Democratic candidate for president is, I pledge to work hard for. I'd like to see Texas turn blue, or at least purple. I want to be a part of that.

Being from El Paso, you've known about Democratic candidate Beto O'Rourke longer than most Americans probably have. What excited you about him?

B: I love how authentic he is. I've gone to his rallies and have had the chance to meet him four different times. When you take a picture with him, afterward he looks you right in the eye.

He laughs and talks like you are a friend. That means more than anything.

Everything he says about El Paso...I love that he loves where he came from. He's very proud of his community and he speaks Spanish. He's got a voice. He is one to watch in the future.

What is it like to live in a state where many people own firearms?

B: It's really horrible. I canvas for political campaigns often and sometimes I think people are going to have their guns when they come to their door. You never know if you're going to piss somebody off and they're going to shoot you, you know? We've been chased and told to leave a neighborhood, that we don't have the right to ask them about voting.

That would turn a lot of people away, I would think, but it sounds like coming up against that kind of resistance actually fuels you. Is that right?

B: Yes, it really does.

Beatriz at Eight Years Old – "Queen of the Catholic Church,"
Juarez, Mexico

Chapter 7

"The Constitutionalist"
Bill

"The Freedom Fighter"
Angie

Bill
"The Constitutionalist"

Born—1947 in Seattle, Washington
Political Identity—Conservative
Constitutionalist

Bill's memories of his early political shaping echoed a common theme heard during other interviews. Many Americans who were alive, or whose parents were alive, during World War II said that political divisions were not as deep as they are in the twenty-first century. Americans were more likely to vote for a candidate based on personality than his or her political party.

While Bill comes from a long line of Democratic family members, his family tree split to the right politically starting with his father once he became a business owner. Bill watched and learned from his father's words and experiences. Bill's father was also a United States Marine Corps veteran and Purple Heart recipient who fought in World War II. His complex views on war helped shape the way Bill went on to resolve conflict in his own life, starting on the schoolyard, and eventually leading him to believe that a mighty defense is the best way to avoid strife globally.

As a college student Bill became increasingly incensed by the anti-war movement during the Vietnam War. While many of his peers grew their hair long, Bill's remained short. He got involved by joining a Young Republicans chapter on campus and has remained passionate about politics ever since.

When did your interest in politics begin?

B: I wasn't that interested until I was in college and I switched from being a pre-med major to a business major. The first class I took at the University of Washington was called "Socialism versus Capitalism." I still remember being assigned an essay where we had to compare and contrast different social and economic systems, specifically a free market versus communist system. We looked at the United States and the U.S.S.R as examples. I couldn't believe the differences! It was the first time I identified as being a Libertarian, with the notion that more freedom is better than less freedom. It also made me want a limited federal government. When government is too involved in our lives we lose freedom, plain and simple.

I wouldn't call myself a true Libertarian though in terms of the economic portion. Libertarians think that they should only support or pay taxes towards those parts of government that they want to support, and I don't agree with that. I also don't think we should only protect our own borders, which true Libertarians believe. Sometimes we need to go offshore to get things stabilized.

JS: The conversation went back to Bill's politically formative college years and the overall tone in the nation while the war in Vietnam intensified.

B: Americans were fighting in Vietnam, but I did not like the anti-war movement, nothing about it. To me being anti-war represented everything anti-American.

It was your generation that was fighting in Vietnam. Did you feel you had more skin in the game than people from other generations at that time?

B: Sure, but most of my generation was actually going socialist and it totally turned me off because socialism may sound wonderful, but there isn't enough money to do it. They were talking about living the communal lifestyle as the only way to go; well I knew that was just a total myth. The whole idea of living in a commune reminded me too much of George Orwell's *Animal Farm*, where you're going to have a leader no matter what. This made a big impact on me, especially the idea that all animals are created equal, but some are more equal than others. I knew exactly where things would lead.

I was also just not into the drug scene. I didn't like the shouting down of anybody that did not agree with you. Everything that anti-war protesters promoted I didn't agree with, and I still don't.

My belief with Vietnam was that we should fight the war and win with honor. It seemed to me that people on the left felt that we should lay down our weapons and walk away. People on the left defended communism by saying that the communists would take what was rightfully theirs and then they'd stop, but I knew that there was no way the communists would ever stop.

Do you think many of your peers leaned left because you lived on the west coast?

B: Yes. The left ideas were moving in and the school of business was on the right.

Did your parents talk with you about politics while you were growing up?

B: They talked with me and my younger brother some about politics, but they weren't all that interested in politics. When my parents were younger a lot of why someone voted had to do with the personality of a candidate more than it was about a candidate's specific viewpoints. For instance, both of my parents voted for Eisenhower because he was a war hero.

Being from a very strong labor family almost everyone in my extended family was a Democrat or was at least brought up that way. It wasn't until my dad became a business owner and started looking at things a little differently, like the way unionization was working, that he became a Republican. My dad didn't think unionization was fair and he felt that the pendulum had swung too far the other way, that instead of making life easier, unions made it harder for him to operate his business. He became irritated because it was hard to get rid of people who weren't doing a good job and at the same time he also found it difficult to reward people who *were* doing a good job.

My dad had a more practical view of unions as a business owner. My mother was more philosophical about them. I remember her comparing unionization to communism; she said things like, "Why should someone work hard if they can't make it to the top?"

That is still one of my biggest beefs with teachers' unions, that they make it so that good teachers aren't paid enough, but bad teachers are paid too much.

JS: Like many war veterans, Bill's father didn't give many de-tails about his time in combat, but he carried a visible reminder —a scar on his temple from a bullet that lodged millimeters from being fatal. Bill remembers that as a child his father imparted what he thought about fighting in general to his two sons. For example, when Bill was in eighth grade he came home crying after being in a fight at school, and he punched another boy in the nose.

B: My dad would often say things along the lines of, "War is a terrible thing, but if something is important enough to fight for, you fight to win."

On the day I came home upset, my dad sat me down and told me to stop my blubbering. He said that I had better never pick a fight, but if someone ever started up with me, I'd better defend myself and make sure I won the fight.

I was surprised then by how anti-war my dad was as I got older and how much he didn't want my brother or me to go to Vietnam. My dad used to say that the first people who should go to war should be the sons of politicians.

JS: When he was eighteen, Bill suffered a seizure. He was diagnosed with epilepsy, which kept him from being drafted.

B: This was the same time I switched majors, from pre-med to business. One of my professors had told me I was more likely to need a doctor than I was to become one. I already had a college deferment, but my dad went down to the Selective Service office to make sure they knew I had epilepsy and then he demanded that they change my draft status. He never told me he did that. I found out years later from someone else.

JS: Meanwhile, Bill's brother, nearly four years younger, went down to the Army recruiting office to enlist so that he could choose to be a helicopter pilot instead of being drafted into an unknown job. This is also how Steve (A World View) made his decision to enlist.

B: My dad marched down to the recruiting office that time and asked if for certain my brother would get to be a helicopter pilot if he enlisted. They hemmed and hawed and said that he would most likely be a mechanic, so my dad told them to tear up the enlistment papers. My brother still got a draft number, but it was low enough that he was never called.

When my dad developed dementia and then Alzheimer's, it was the first time he ever talked about the war with us and how horrible it was. It was really crushing to hear.

Do you remember if you were influenced by extended family members who were Democrats?

B: My (maternal) grandfather was a politician. He had been the Mayor of Seattle and was of the old school—totally party politics. You voted strict party lines, period. He believed that if a candidate had a "D" next to his name you voted for him. If he had an "R" then you should send him off to jail.

I voted for Richard Nixon in 1968 when he ran against Hubert Humphrey. Oh my god, when I told my grandfather I voted for Nixon, he turned beet red. He looked at me with so much contempt and said, "At least I know my vote canceled yours!"

I didn't know he felt quite so strong, to tell you the truth. He made me think I didn't understand the issues involved.

Why did you choose to vote for Nixon in 1968?

B: One of the big reasons was that Nixon gave the indication that he knew how to solve the war in Vietnam. Humphrey didn't seem to have any idea what was going on over there and (outgoing President) Lyndon B. Johnson had not done a damn thing, in my opinion.

Why do you identify as a constitutionalist?

B: I believe that the Constitution was written for a reason and that it was written with the idea that it is a rock. Not that it is infallible or can't ever be changed, but it should only be changed through a real super majority, otherwise it would be too whimsical. And most of the framers, what they were afraid of, was mob rule. That's why I go absolutely nuts with this whole concept of one person, one vote when it comes to the Upper House of the Legislature. That is one of the reasons there are supposed to be two Houses. One should be based strictly on population and that is why we have the Census every ten years.

The other Legislative House should be based upon state's rights, but this has largely been changed so that the preponderance of all representation to the state government comes from large, liberal areas. So what happens is the different ideas for every county are not really being represented.

JS: Bill described what the phrase "drain the swamp" means to him, a metaphor popularized by then-candidate Donald Trump during the 2016 election.

B: I believe the way that the senators on the federal level run now is that since they have a six year term, they can pretty much do any damn thing that they want for four or five years and then go out and lie about it, and do nothing other than get re-elected. They likely will. There's only about a ten percent turnover rate with politicians.

What do you think people can do about that?

B: To change this, people need to actually know what it says in our Constitution and understand some of the reasons behind what is in it. One of the big reasons behind our Constitution was the idea that village rule, or local governments, should lead. Instead the federal government has taken on a larger and larger role.

Many people want to see the Electoral College system changed. Do you believe in the Electoral College the way it runs now because it is in the Constitution or because you think it is a good check in terms of checks and balances?

B: I believe the Electoral College is a great check. It gives every state a certain amount of participation in the system. If you only had it based upon popular vote, again you can safely bet that the east and west coasts would determine what happens in the rest of the country. The framers of the Constitution didn't want to have rule by popular opinion because popular opinion can change dramatically in a relatively short period of time.

When I look at the Constitution it's amazing to me that the framers could be that smart and that forward thinking. If you want to change it, fine, but do it the way it's supposed to be changed.

Do you worry about any potential changes to the Constitution?

B: Am I worried that a president could say global warming is the biggest threat to the world? Maybe. But I know they will never touch the second amendment.

What do you think would make America thrive? Is there a way that you think could bring about unity?

B: I think all adult citizens should do something that would benefit the country and make them feel part of it. I think it would be great if every man and woman could learn more about our country by being in some kind of organization like the military or the Peace Corps and serve at least two years. We had an exchange student from Switzerland when I was in high school and that's when I learned that Switzerland has a mandatory military expectation for its citizens. I think it's a great idea.

JS: Switzerland has mandatory military service for all physically healthy male citizens under age fifty, though women may volunteer. This basic military service is for approximately five months and some additional training is required throughout adulthood.

B: I also think every young person should learn how to use a firearm. If schools are going to teach sex education, they should teach how to safely use a firearm. I think it's important so that people aren't frightened, or enamored, by guns. When I was twelve or thirteen my brother and I went to NRA (National Rifle Association) safety classes. The first thing they taught us was how to check to see if a gun is loaded. The second was that you never point the barrel of a gun at anybody, whether it's loaded or not. It definitely taught me how to safely use a firearm.

I also think two things need to be taught in schools: civics and American history, not revisionist history which we see today. Revisionist history is when people revise history based on standards now versus standards during another time. For instance, some people want to remove monuments devoted to our Founding Fathers because of things that were a standard part of their past, such as being slave owners. All of this revisionist history we're seeing in schools today worries me.

I also think that really learning civics and economics will give young people a greater love for our country; it sure did for me. When I was growing up in the 1950s and 1960s we learned how our state and federal governments work. This was when I was eight years old through high school. I think it's harmed the country that civics isn't taught in public schools anymore. Now children are being taught that the Unites States is a bad country. This attitude has destroyed things more than it has helped.

What students should be taught instead is that Russia and China are our biggest threats.

I worry as much about an economic war with Russia or China as much as a military war with them. They're communist countries, but they've allowed people to share in the wealth. People are benefiting from their own labor, which is not the way communist systems work. What scares me is to see Russia and China taking part in the free market system while their military is growing fast. Once they think they are the same or better than us, we are in big trouble.

People from all over the world want to come to the United States because we are not a socialist country. As young as our country is, we are the longest lasting democracy in the world…It has been one great experiment.

Angie
"The Freedom Fighter"

Born—1978 in Czestochowa, Poland
Political Identity—Ultra-Conservative but
Registered Independent

Stories of Angie's parents' passage to the United States have been a part of their family story for as long as Angie can recall. She was two years old when her mother and father emigrated from Poland, fresh college graduates who had lived with their baby daughter in campus housing before deciding to embark on their dream with their only child. The young family left all of their loved ones behind to come to California, the Golden State. The story has come to symbolize freedom and Angie's version of the American Dream. After living with a sponsor until they could make it on their own, Angie's parents went on to do what many Americans consider ordinary: they secured jobs, purchased a car, and then bought a home in the suburbs. All were extraordinary to them, however. Angie distinctly recalled the momentous day when the family signed their new citizenship papers together, the culmination of their American Dream.

Angie's political shaping started around the dinner table as a young girl, when her parents railed against the pitfalls of living in a communist country. While Angie discussed her political beliefs throughout our conversation it was clear that in her opinion the antonym to "freedom" is "communism."

Angie lives in the San Francisco Bay Area where, she explained, she's been stigmatized for being a Trump supporter. A single woman, Angie said her politics have even affected her dating life. While a self-described "ultra conservative" when it comes to most issues, Angie explained that she is a registered Independent so that she doesn't miss any candidates who may enter a race.

Angie believes that the country is at a critical juncture leading up to the 2020 national elections and the issues that she feels are most in jeopardy center around freedom of religion and the defense of legal immigration policies.

What made your parents decide to leave Poland?

A: They wanted to leave a communist regime. It was a very difficult life for them in Poland. The government ran absolutely everything. There were food rations and just overall a lot of corruption. Even though they were educated, there were no economic opportunities whatsoever for my parents in Poland. They always described it to me as just a bleak future.

My parents met in college. I even lived in their dorm room for a year! One of the big reasons that they wanted to come to the U.S. was that they both graduated college and had degrees in engineering, which they knew would give them opportunities in the U.S.

Did anyone else from their families come to the United States with them?

A: No. My dad says it was all because of my mom that the three of us came. She was hell-bent on going to the United States, which was a dream come true for many people in Poland at that time. They felt like America was a land far, far away. A lot of people talked about going to America, but not many actually did it.

My mom was twenty-four and my dad was twenty-six. They applied for political asylum as refugees, kind of like all the talk that is going on at our border now. They did the whole application process the way you're supposed to do it. They were approved to go to Austria first, where they lived in a refugee camp for two months with me, which was totally crazy. From there they got visas through the Catholic Church to come to the United States.

They got to pick between North Carolina, California, Texas, and New York. They thought, "Hey if we're going to the U.S., we'll go to California."

Our sponsor family was a nice family that volunteered through the church to take political refugees. We lived with them for three months in the Bay Area, in the city of Danville.

Luckily my parents had an education. Within a few months my dad got a job with Bechtel in San Francisco, which was amazing. We moved out of the sponsor family's home and rented an apartment. My mom was not working yet because she was still learning English.

JS: When Angie was four years old her maternal grandmother emigrated to the United States as well and lived with the family, caring for Angie while her mom went to work as an engineer, also.

A: We didn't have a car, so I remember that we took the bus or we walked everywhere. I remember when we got a car it was a big deal—it was very exciting. When my parents finally bought a house in a sub-development it was like our American Dream came true.

How did your parents impress that idea of the American Dream upon you?

A: When you're coming from a communist country, most people don't understand what that really is because they've had no experience with it. Even if their parents or grandparents have experienced what it is really like to live in a communist country, they aren't able to share what it's like.

If someone were to do their homework on what a communistic country is truly like, it's pretty horrific. The government controls everything—whoever works for the government has money and maybe a small percentage of people at the top do too, but basically everyone is poor. There is no middle class and whether you're a janitor or a doctor you make the same income.

What issues make you identify as a conservative?

A: Immigration is a big one. My parents stood in line and immigrated the way it's supposed to be done. I agree with President Trump's stance on merit-based immigration. My parents worked hard for everything. They probably wouldn't have made it as well as they did in the U.S. if they didn't come educated and ready to have good jobs. (Immigration officials) definitely looked at all of that back then. My parents were never on any sort of public assistance, ever. They always instilled in me that you get what you work for, not what you wish for.

I remember the day I got my U.S. citizenship at the same time as my parents. I was eight years old and we went to San Francisco to sign our naturalization proof of citizenship documents, which I still have.

Do you always vote for Republican candidates?

A: I am a registered Independent, but I tend to vote Republican.

What principles make you align more with the Republican party?

A: Communist rulers want a secular society; instead of religion, they want the people's higher power to be the government. But if you are a religious person, then you believe your rights come from God, and that God has a plan for your life.

Our Founding Fathers put in the Constitution that life, liberty, and the pursuit of happiness and freedom are God given rights; they are not government given. Everyone should have the opportunity to pursue life, liberty, and the pursuit of happiness, but if you don't have freedom, you don't get to have those things.

So you see the Republican party as representing freedom more than the Democratic party does?

A: Yes, because the more the government runs, the fewer freedoms people have. With a capitalist economy and a Democratic country, there is a lot of personal freedom…to start a business, do a side hustle, to make a lot of money. My parents are an example of this.

The government is supposed to be limited; that's what Republicans believe.

When you start sliding into socialism it's an in between, where the government starts running more and more, and more and more. Slowly you start having less and less freedom, which we can already see happening in California. California is the most left state in the country and if you go to other states you realize how regulated things are in California.

My tax lady told me how even though she offered to take in her blood related niece, her niece ended up in foster care. The state of California denied her as guardian because she had built a room in her house without a permit. Are you kidding me? That, to me, is communism. You go to other states and it is not like that yet.

Are you actively involved in politics?

A: I wish I could, but there are not a lot of opportunities for Republican women in the Bay Area. For now, I pay a lot of attention.

What makes you care about politics so much?

A: What's going on in the world affects us. It's important. When I was growing up that's what everyone talked about at the dinner table. I grew up believing that one of the worst things a person could do was to not know what's going on.

How is it being a conservative in a blue state?

A: I'm single so I date, but you can't be an open conservative in the Bay Area. I can't tell you how often someone has written on their profile, "If you're a Trump supporter, swipe left. Don't message me. Not interested."

I've seen it many, many, many times. I guess they can tell by my profile, but I have also had people message me to ask, "Are you a Trump supporter?"

And I've said, "Yes, that's who I voted for."

They said, "We're done here."

It blows my mind when people do this because I know that there are good people on the left. I just don't agree with their policies.

You don't say "not interested" if you know upfront that someone on a dating site supports a Democrat for president?

A: I would definitely not in a million years. If they looked attractive or cool based on their profile, how they vote would never stop me from meeting them. I'd want to sit down face to face and I'm sure I'd find that there's a lot that we *do* agree on.

I'll be honest. I can talk about issues and not make it personal, but I only find that hard-core hate in my experience from the left. I don't really see it from people on the right.

Where do you think that anger comes from in your experience?

A: I've thought about that. I don't believe either side, right or left, is pristine white. That's not possible. We're dealing with human beings, but the left seems to be intolerant, almost hateful, to people who are conservative. It's like, "If you don't think the way I think, you're a racist, you're a bigot."

Well I know I'm not. I know my family is not. I still don't agree with where you fall on the issues.

Do you believe this country is on the right track? What is your American Dream for yourself, for society?

A: I don't think Trump is perfect, but I like a lot of his policies, like his stance on legal immigration. I think if Trump gets booted out of office we've lost the country, I really do. I think democracy is done if that happens.

The second amendment is very important and it's something else that people don't understand. The Founding Fathers put the second amendment in the Constitution not so that people can hunt and fish, although that's great, but the Founding Fathers knew that people need guns to protect themselves from the government.

Every time you have a government where the only people who can have guns work for the government, it's usually a communist regime, or close to one, or it's a dictatorship and people die. It's a dangerous situation. It's not a conversation that's had because even in public schools our children aren't taught about communism, about how it happens and what it brings.

We fought wars to get rid of communism. The fact that people are even dabbling in the rhetoric of it...the things that Bernie Sanders says sometimes are straight out of the

"Communist Manifesto," seriously. Some of the 2020 presidential candidates, the things they say are communist beliefs down to the wire.

Why do you think some of the 2020 candidates' platforms are further left than we've seen?

A: If I had to guess, one would be the immigration problem. They think they are helping, but in reality, a lot of people are looking around and don't recognize our country anymore because of our current immigration policies.

My parents were very proud of being Polish Americans, but they assimilated to be American. It is wonderful to visit a Polish section in a city, like in Chicago. That's good immigration, that's healthy. But today immigrants don't say, "I can't wait to be an American." That's gone and I think it's unsettling. It's robbed us of an American culture.

I think for whatever reason the left is also not pro-family. They want government to replace a lot of things where the family should be responsible instead.

In what ways do you think government has tried to replace family?

A: I was watching this town hall in Chicago on Fox News. This area in Chicago is like a war zone. It's a four-block radius that's predominantly African American and there are more deaths and shootings there than in Afghanistan. At the town hall there were cops, families, pastors…talking about what's going on and why it's gotten so bad in this part of Chicago. Now if you watch the media the problem is always guns. But a pastor said that the real problem is that like ninety percent of these young men have grown up without a father. Another black leader also said that at one point the welfare system gave black men an out to take care of their kids. This is a controversial statement, but I believe there's an element of truth to it.

It just seems like many policies of the left really don't support families, religion, or faith.

Socialism really is a gradual stepping-stone to communism. How you do it is by slowly chipping away at people's freedoms, slowly so that they don't notice. That has already been happening. The government is controlling more and more and more.

Do you think it's malicious intent, or just another way of looking at the world?

A: The people at the top know exactly what they're doing, but most people don't know, they don't know. These young adults who want Bernie Sanders for president and think it's a cool thing, they don't know what living in a socialist country is really like.

How do we reconcile the polar opposite ideologies of what's best for our country? Where can we find solutions?

A: My theory is that until Trump came along there was a lot of corruption. All of Washington, the Democrats and the Republicans, were left to do whatever they wanted. A lot of those politicians are really wealthy. No one really knows how they made all of that money. They don't get paid as much as they're worth. That was "the swamp."

Now with Trump in office, he's no saint, but we know what we're getting. He doesn't hide it. There are people on the left who will stop at nothing to get him out of office because it's possible that they're not white as the driven snow. They don't want more corruption to come out.

Are there any candidates you've been excited about?

A: A lot of conservatives were jumping up and down in 2016. I was really glad when Trump won and I'm still really glad Trump won. No one can deny that what Trump has done with the economy has been amazing - that was all him. He's very good about business and money; he knows about the stock market. I think if Hillary won it would be a very bleak deal.

I don't like the way Trump talks; it creates more problems. The tweets, it's just drama, but that's who he is. If Trump could turn into Mike Pence in terms of his demeanor...

In my opinion the main reason Trump was elected was because of his stance on immigration, period. It was like, finally, we have somebody who is saying out loud that if we don't do something about illegal immigration we are going to lose the country. I think that's why he won.

If Trump doesn't get re-elected, we're going to get four to eight years of socialist change, and I think that is frightening. For these reasons I will for sure be voting for Trump again.

Angie and Her Parents

Chapter 8

"The Messenger"
Todd

"The Brave"
Lauren

Todd
The Messenger

Born—1987 in
Placerville, California
Political Identity—Conservative

JULIE SAMRICK

Todd still lives in the area in which he was born and raised, a rural Sierra Nevada foothills community between Sacramento and Lake Tahoe. Todd's parents also grew up there, high school sweethearts who went on to raise three sons in a home where politics may have not been emphasized, but hard work was. As a boy Todd was active in 4-H and the Future Farmers of America—national youth organizations that use agricultural education to teach young people skills like leadership. He carried values that were instilled in him as a child into adulthood, including the value of community and a belief that the best kind of communication is sitting down casually with someone for a slice of pie and a cup of coffee.

While he was growing up, Todd said his parents seemed to identify more with the Democratic Party because of its pro-union, working party connotation. Todd, however, became increasingly interested in politics and by high school he joined his school's Young Liberals club.

Todd recalled being a freshman in high school on September 11, 2001, a date he noted as a turning point in his political shaping. As the country watched in horror in the days following the attack, Todd remembered being drawn to President George W. Bush's response, thinking of him for the first time as a strong leader, as Todd's preferred leader, after the contested 2000 Presidential Election.

While talking with Todd, it became clear that he is fueled by his interactions with others. The more people he talks with in his community, the more Todd has been led to take action regarding political causes. Not long after he graduated from college, Todd campaigned for a seat on his former high school district's board of trustees and won. Todd currently serves as the chairman of his county's Republican Party. Once he learns about different issues affecting the people in his greater community, Todd wants to do more, and to know more. He is active while holding down a full-time job at a non-profit organization.

Todd comes across as informed and invested. He is motivated to turn his blue state red, describing why he thinks conservative policies would return California to its former glory. Todd discussed a range of issues affecting the state, from California's public school system, to sanctuary city laws, to the way language is used on ballots in order to sway voters.

While Todd shared what he thinks is going well in the rest of the country, the national deficit concerns him. Todd believes the Republican Party should accept some responsibility for it and do more to prioritize getting out of debt.

What has led you to believe as you do, politically?

T: When I was growing up we lived on acreage. We raised animals and my parents always encouraged us to find work and even side jobs. My dad was a sheet metal foreman. He and my mom voted more on the candidates than they voted strictly on party. They weren't registered in a political party, but I would say they were more on the liberal side when I was growing up. I used to think Republicans were only rich people.

When I started high school I got involved with the Young Liberal club. I was a freshman in high school on 9/11 and from that day on my political beliefs started to slowly transition. I stayed in the Young Liberal club for a while, but I remember being impressed by President George W. Bush. After seeing his response, I couldn't imagine Al Gore being our President.

I slowly became a Republican and eventually started to view the Democrat Party as the party that wanted to give everything away to people without asking them to work for it. When I turned eighteen, I registered as a Republican. I'm still Republican at this point, and now that the Democratic Party has gone so far left, I don't know if I'll ever return to it.

You must be politically minded in general if you've felt strongly enough to be involved with both parties at times.

T: Yes, I've always been active in politics. Since I was a kid I have kept up on what's going on locally, statewide, and nationally. I think that my involvement in politics is a by-product of being active in the community. It might be that I get involved with the cemetery district or the park district, but I find that once I get active in one area, it leads me to getting involved in even more issues.

You were elected to your local school board when you were in your twenties. When did you first take a leadership position?

T: Growing up I was involved with the Future Farmers of America and I was active in 4-H. Through 4-H I formed an advocacy group called Youth Coming Together. When I was in high school I got a grant from Kraft Foods to do a documentary on hunger issues in my county. I traveled all around, talking to different people, and we showed our video to a lot of different schools. Our advocacy group became my county's Youth Commission, which still exists today. I was its first chairperson.

What were some of the issues your Youth Commission worked on?

T: Our main issue was that a group of people wanted to shut down a neighborhood skate park and fill it with sand. We held a community forum and advocated to our Board of Supervisors and they solved the issue.

What is your role as the chair of your county's Republican Party?

T: It's not a real flashy position. I interact with volunteers and I try to get people organized. I see what issues people are talking about and give feedback to my counterparts, through my other community involvements. We talk about a whole litany of issues. We just had a forum about homelessness; we've advocated for affordable fire insurance and forest fuel reduction. Our big issue right now is advocating for Prop 13.

JS: Proposition 13 was passed in 1978 and later upheld by the U.S. Supreme Court to limit property taxes on California real estate to not exceed a two percent increase each year. It is officially named the People's Initiative to Limit Property Taxation. A large contributor to its passing was the sentiment that older Californians should not be priced out of their homes through high taxes. In 2020 it is on the state ballot to repeal Prop. 13, which Todd believes would be a disaster.

Why do you align more with the Republican Party?

T: The reason I'm a Republican is because I think that California has become a one-party state that doesn't seem to want to do anything about crime or homelessness. Those issues are exacerbated by welfare and a kind of complacency among people. California's Democratic leaders even, in fact, view what they're doing as an accomplishment and it just breaks my heart because I am so in love with California.

As the chair of my county's Republican Party, I talk to people every single week who are moving out of California. I almost feel like California is dying a slow death and something has got to give. But we can't give up on California, we just can't.

What can be done to improve things in your opinion?

T: I think reducing taxes, decreasing regulations, streamlining budgets, emphasizing personal responsibility and property rights, for God's sake. We need to protect Prop. 13 and make it easier for people to buy a home. Those are all things that need to happen in order to make California a good place to live again. I don't see (Governor) Gavin Newsom doing anything about it. That's why I'm a Republican.

What would California look like if it is lost?

T: I think about this every day, several times a day, all day. It's something that's constantly on my mind. I go through the stages of grief.

JS: Todd laughed at this point from his hyperbole, but really does struggle with what he thinks is his state's decline.

T: I can't imagine, with cops being so disrespected and gas prices so high and the criminals running amok, this going on forever. I have a good team at the Republican Central Committee. We have this perpetual hope that things will get better because it wasn't that long ago that the state recalled (former Governor) Gray Davis.

California is worth fighting for. It has to be fought for. With a state of forty million people you can't just say, "Well I'm getting out."

I am single and I don't have children, so it's a little easier for me to get by, but I often have conversations with members of our local community who have families and children. It's getting hard for them to stay in California. This should be something that the rest of the nation should care about because you can't have a state as big as California and not have it affect the rest of the country. When things implode in California it's going to spread nationwide.

Do you have hope for California?

T: We have Republican leadership on the state level that has complained about how bad things are getting, and they are just starting to do something about it. I think if we advocate and really show people what the Republican Party is doing for the middle class, I think we can gain some ground.

Do I think we'll be the majority in the state? No, but if we get back a sizable minority then we can work from there. If we get three more Senate seats back in the state Legislature, we can basically create a lame duck governor. Any party needs a two-thirds majority in the state to do anything; we just need to take that back.

How would you do this?

T: I think it will be hard work, but we can do it. It's a ground game. The Republican Party needs to demonstrate through social media a real cause and effect. They need to go to the pillars of every business community, the mom and pop shops, the local bars that everyone knows about. Tell these people what the local policies are doing to them. We have to start reaching out to immigrant communities. Immigrants from Vietnam and other Asian communities come to California with nothing, start businesses, and are thriving. Those business owners, those new people to the country, are the new Republicans.

Why do you think people are leaving California?

T: We need to get real about the cost of living in the state of California. It is a good labor market, but a lot of people are moving out of state because it's expensive. People want to come here, but they become stuck between a rock and a hard place. I think if they can find a good job out of state, they'll move, and people are doing that.

Many other policies are also getting worse in California. Whenever you have one party controlling everything, they do things to fit their purposes and not the people's purposes. California is a prime example of that. The Democrats have a super majority in both Houses. They have San Francisco and Los Angeles; they have the votes that they need, so there is a feeling that they don't care about rural communities.

So, it's not necessarily the policies of the Democratic Party you take issue with than it is the super majority taking over?

T: I think it is in both their policies and that they have the power in state government to control everything. I think people deserve a balance.

Why do you think so many people in California are registered Democrats then?

T: Even though the Democrats have a huge majority of registered voters, the fastest growing political preference in California is "decline-to-state." There are more decline-to-state voters than there are registered Republicans. I think people are getting really dissatisfied with both political parties and are declining to state because they want to vote based on the person and not the party.

The only problem with having decline-to-state voters is that state and national politics are based on party. I think that we need to demonstrate to those who decline to affiliate with a political party what the Republican Party is doing and show our way forward. We need to show that we want to preserve Prop 13; we want to be a state that protects law and order and a decent way of life. Criminals can't harm or kill innocent people and get away with it. You can't tell me that the majority of people are okay with someone like Kate Steinle's killer, who was an illegal alien, and shot her in the face.

JS: Steinle was a 32-year-old woman who was murdered in 2015 while walking in a tourist section of San Francisco with her father. The case has since become a hot topic of issues surrounding immigration and sanctuary city laws.

Todd also blamed the way language is used on state ballots for swaying election outcomes.

T: Voters are also manipulated because of the way California's Attorney General words the language on ballots for various propositions, making the language sound so different from what the laws would actually mean if enacted. People are so busy that they don't have the time to research. So, when voters see the title "The Safe Schools and Community Act," which was Prop. 47, they don't realize that that lowers the penalty for crimes like the rape of an unconscious victim from a felony to a misdemeanor. People thought they were voting to keep their schools and communities safe by voting when in reality they were letting violent offenders out on the street. It's this manipulation of information and outright lying that really needs to stop.

Prop. 6 was to repeal the gas tax, but it was called the "Repeal of Transportation Funding." Who wants to repeal that? They are manipulating the vote and gerrymandering these districts, and it's not right.

It should be criminal, but ballot harvesting is legal. You should never allow people to collect other people's ballots. That's one of the major reasons we went from fourteen Congressional seats down to seven Congressional seats in California.

I have to remember though, that as liberal as people think California is, it voted Republican in every presidential election between 1952 and 1988. We passed the Three Strikes Law in the 1990s. We voted against affirmative action in 1996 and outlawed it in our university and hiring practices.

What do you think is going right and wrong on both state and national levels?

T: Nationally I think the economy is moving; unemployment levels are great. I think we're finally getting a handle on China and their outright stealing of our intellectual property and our trade. I think our Supreme Court is getting some Justices on it who interpret the Constitution and what it says, instead of what they want it to say. I think the President, even though he is abrasive at times, is actually very direct with the American people and I think we have more of an inside view into what goes on behind the scenes because of him than we've ever had before.

What I think is going wrong is that the national deficit is still a disgrace. I think we have a government on both sides of the aisle spending money like drunken sailors and I think we're doing our children and grandchildren no favors in that regard. We really need to cut. The Republicans have not cut on a national level and that's been going on for a long time. We need to remember we are the party of limited government. We can't have limited government if we are increasing the size of it continually. That's what we're guilty of. I think the national debt is one of the big things that will severely harm us, but no one wants to talk about because all politicians love to spend money. The state of California is the same way.

JS: Todd had a lot to say about California's public school system, especially its public college system.

T: As for what's going right in the state of California? I can't think of one thing that is going right. I think the education system in our state is a travesty. We have seen a return of admitting people to our universities based on what they look like or where they came from instead of what they're accomplishing. You see lower performing students getting into universities based on perceived race, income, and citizenship status, instead of what their merits are or how well they perform. That is not good. We need to take back the education system, from kindergarten through high school and college.

Continually things are seeping through that have nothing to

do with creating more engineers, or things that are going to keep us competitive. We are competing with China and India, places that could give a rip about making sure their schools have a diverse make-up. They don't care what color you are, what gender you are, or where you came from. They care about how you perform. Those countries are just churning out people that will work in the tech industry and other industries that will increase our gross domestic product.

In the University of California system we are seeing a rise in social sciences. Although that has its place, those are not competitive fields. Instead our universities are discussing gender, race, and Western civilization in a context that bashes it and bashes the capitalistic way of life.

It blows my mind that we live in the wealthiest country the world has ever seen and a way of life that allows people to make their own decisions and to elect their own representatives, and yet we have an education system in California, and really in much of the country, that just pounds on that way of life and wants to see it done away with. Our education system has been totally taken over in the state by people who are dedicated socialists, by and large.

The University of California system is so overfunded and advocates ideals that are not congruent with the free way of life, and that has to change. It has to change or we are not going to be around as a country much longer. We'll be around, but we won't recognize what's made this country great.

This country was made by people who came here with nothing, but who worked hard and sacrificed everything. This country was not made by intellectual elites. It was made up by people who were not well educated or from wealthy families. They weren't professors, or people you find at expensive dinner parties. They were just down to earth people who made this country up. We need to realize that and respect our history. We've made our errors, but this country has done a pretty good job for people.

Have you always voted Republican?

T: On a state and federal level I have. On a local level I have voted for people from both parties.

Do you think we are at a turning point?

T: I think we're at a time of great conflict. I've never seen so much polarization among people. I think we need to look at things for what they are. People need to take the time to drill down and research for themselves what things are and how they got to be that way and I think looking at history is a great way to do that. If you understand history, you understand what's happening. Every civilization that's been powerful, if they forget who they are, that's when they dissipate. As Americans, we need to remember who we are.

Todd Speaking at a Chamber of Commerce Event

Lauren
"The Brave"

Born—1975 in
Rochester, New York
Political Identity—Progressive

When Lauren didn't like what was happening in her community, she ran for a city council seat in 2018 and won. She continued carrying the torch that her grandmother lit nearly a century ago, which was reignited in her daughter, Lauren's mother, and then her granddaughter.

As a young child Lauren, her older sister, and their parents moved from upstate New York to a suburb in Los Angeles County, where Lauren said she had a childhood that was "sheltered" and "privileged." Lauren's maternal grandparents moved west as well, settling close to Lauren and her family. Political discourse was at the center of family get-togethers. As though through osmosis, the older women's politics seeped through to Lauren, though she didn't act on those principles for years to come.

As much as anything, Lauren's Jewish identity has contributed to her political shaping. I was fascinated to hear Lauren describe how her faith and her politics intersect.

It took a lack of leadership in Lauren's local government to propel her to make change as an adult. She hasn't looked back since she was sworn into office in 2018. Like Todd, (The Messenger), Lauren takes a grassroots approach, aiming to spread a message that the policies she believes in are the best course for her new home state of Texas and the United States at large. Like Todd, Lauren takes issue with the structure of government and where she thinks powers get stacked unfairly. Lauren believes the word "progressive" has gotten a negative connotation and she seeks to change it. Instead of the country moving far left, Lauren believes the truth is really that it has moved far right. She believes her progressive vision for America makes plain common sense and she is focused on doing her part to shift a red state blue, much like Todd is working to change his blue state red. In the meantime, Lauren says she will settle for purple.

What is your earliest political shaping memory?

L: With my mom and her family, everything was about politics. You couldn't have a conversation without politics. As a child I thought it was exhausting and boring when they talked about politics. My grandmother talked about speaking at different groups and about various organizations she was involved in. She was always very ahead of her time, a forward-thinking person. She talked about things like universal healthcare back in the 1980s.

My grandmother had been a teacher and a union organizer in New York City in the 1940s. She earned a bachelor's degree in chemistry when she was only nineteen. This was at a time when most women didn't go to college, let alone major in anything outside of a teaching degree.

How do you think your grandmother's own political beliefs were shaped?

L: My grandparents were well traveled, and they saw different political systems at work. As a labor organizer my grandmother saw how the lives of workers could be improved. She became a dedicated political activist. My mom was as well. When I was a child my mom was always working on campaigns and donating to causes. That was always a foundation for my thinking.

We were typical, liberal, American Jews. By that I mean our family is educated, engaged, and politically liberal, which is typical of the American Jewish community.

JS: When pressed for more clarification, Lauren explained what she views as principle differences between the Democrat and Republican Parties.

L: American Jews tend to be Democratic, pretty liberal. The orthodox community isn't so much, but that's a small proportion of us. Jewish people in general don't respond much to authority or following a leader blindly. It's not a solid line community. We're supposed to question; we're supposed to study. We're supposed to interpret and not just follow instruction. For thousands of years, going back to the Talmud, which is the book where all of the Jewish scholars of yesteryear put their interpretation of the Torah, Jews have argued, and that was expected. There wasn't one right answer. Many different interpretations are put in the Talmud, unlike other religions where there is one person at the hierarchy, at the top, who says, "This is the interpretation."

The Jewish community doesn't work that way. From my perspective that contributes to the liberal political leanings.

From my perspective conservatives have more faith in their leadership and tend to fall in line; they question less. These days that often looks like faith in religion as truth. Whereas when you're dealing with liberals, everybody has their own perspective and they're going to argue what the right way is, so it's like herding cats. I think this is why it's harder for liberals to raise money and to get elected because they have to get more people to support them.

I believe that conservatives tend to follow a more hierarchical, authoritarian system where with liberals everyone is on the same playing field. Everyone has their own point of view. To organize that is nearly impossible. That is why I think some very Christian conservatives have drifted to conservative politics even though a lot of Christianity doesn't agree with conservative politics. Because it's faith-based. It's not just faith in God, but faith in leaders.

When and why did you eventually get involved in politics?

L: I always had it in the background and knew it was important to my mother and grandmother, but politics didn't really touch my life. I didn't really get interested in politics until 2015 when Hilary Clinton and Donald Trump were in the (2016 presidential) race.

I was always involved in volunteer work, back to when I was in high school and then in college. When I look back I see that there has always been a sustainability thread throughout my adult life. It changed my perspective on things when I learned about sustainability in housing and landscaping as an adult. This started in the 1990s, before climate change was a common conversation. Today sustainability is always top of mind for me.

JS: Lauren came up against what she called her Texas town's "very restrictive solar ordinances" after she and her husband got solar panels put on their roof several years ago.

L: Our city council had a rule that homeowners couldn't have solar panels on any street view. For this reason it was difficult, depending on the way a house is oriented, to utilize solar panels. I started working to get that ordinance removed and went to the city council with expert witnesses, petitions, data, and studies, showing solar panels increase property values.

The city council unanimously voted to retain the ordinance, basically because they think being able to see solar panels is unattractive. It was this rude, eye-opening moment for me because I didn't change the perspective of one single person sitting up there. They voted as a unit that ignored all of my data and it was very frustrating.

JS: Lauren was confounded when it happened again.

L: We had another issue come up where thousands of people were asking the city council to do something different than they were deciding, and again the council unanimously decided to do it anyway. I was so frustrated that there was nobody representing our perspective at our local level.

JS: Instead of sitting at home and complaining, Lauren decided to become part of the political process and enact change. She ran for a city council seat in 2018 and won. She campaigned on issues surrounding sustainability and supporting the less fortunate.

L: I had no plans to run for council. Three days before the filing deadline someone asked me if I would. I talked with my husband and he said, "That might be a good idea."

With his input and the input of others, I filed two days later with no plan and no money. I had nothing. City council is a short race. You file in February and the election is in May. I had two months to work my butt off. In Texas, voter turn-out for local elections is incredibly low. In city council elections it's about getting people to the polls. My city has about 105,000 people and of those there are 60,000 voters. If you can get 1,600 voters out of 3,000 to the polls, then you'll win. So it's not a mandate for you if you do win; it's just a numbers game.

My husband and I went all in. I had forty-one percent of the vote out of three candidates. The other two were conservatives. I won by forty-four votes in a run-off.

Do you live in a blue city?

L: My little area of town is probably the bluest part, but I'd say it's a purple city.

What took you from California to Texas?

L: Our rent in California was the same as our mortgage in Texas—that's why a lot of people move here.

How is it to live in a red state as a progressive?

L: Texas takes conservatism to a whole new level, but I deserve to enjoy where I live as much as anyone who is a fifth generation Texan. When the population changes, so should the culture. But a lot of people in Texas don't believe that at all-they think, "If you're going to move to Texas, you better learn how to be a Texan."

We have a group of billionaire donors who basically run the show here. They're called "Empower Texans." They are basically the financiers behind the state Tea Party and it's made up of only five or six guys. They are Dominionists. They have a vision for this country that is not what the majority of this country wants. They want to turn this country into a Christian nation and they are making a lot of headway in Texas and it's really scary. I know minorities in Texas are afraid.

Although you're in North Texas, is what the media shows about detention centers in Texas true in your opinion?

L: They are putting citizens in detention centers. There is no due process. They are deporting people without judge and jury trials. We are talking about true authoritarian stuff that is happening in this state under the guise of the federal government. The state leadership is absolutely in favor of it. There is unconstitutional stuff happening every single day in this state and they are quite happy about it. We have a big population of liberal people in Texas, but again, it's not proportional representation here. If it were, and the voter suppression tactics they used were abolished, we would be a blue state.

Take me back to 2015. How did Hilary Clinton's campaign shape or affirm your beliefs?

L: I've always been a Democrat. I've always been a voter. It wasn't that I didn't participate in the political process, I just didn't want to talk about it or be particularly active outside of voting. What I think excited me was the possibility of a female president. It was like, "Oh my God, this might really happen." I didn't campaign for her, but I knew I'd vote for her and it actually looked like she was going to win. It was very exciting for women across the country.

Do any other elections or candidates stand out during your lifetime?

L: I really liked Obama.

What issues make you align with the Democratic Party?

L: Almost every issue. Economic justice, environmental justice, criminal justice. Probably every issue now I align with the progressive wing of the Democratic Party. To me they (progressives) look at outcomes and say, "This is where we want to be—how do we get there?"

To me our country is very far behind a lot of the rest of the modern world. Oftentimes the solution has already been given in another country. All we have to do is model ourselves in that particular issue after that country.

I think it is ridiculous when progressives are called "socialists" or "super-far-left." All we're trying to do is catch up to other countries that we consider to be our peers, other places like England and France, Canada and Israel. They have these social systems that we don't have. We're just trying to catch up. If you actually look at the true political spectrum, progressive politics are pretty moderate. It's just that our politics (in the United States) have skewed so far to the right that progressive policies sound like socialism, but they're not at all. When you poll issues instead of people across the American population, progressive issues poll very well. When you poll gun reform it polls in the ninetieth percentile. This is not socialism. This is not authoritarian regimes taking away your weapons. This is common sense. This is a moderate policy.

When you poll healthcare for all, specifically healthcare as a right, it also polls very high across the entire country because it is a common sense legislation. It is a moderate, normal concept.

When you poll criminal justice reform it polls well across the country because it's one of those things that just makes sense and the outcomes are better than what we have, and it works in other countries. For instance, the death penalty—we're like the only western country that still has the death penalty.

We're one of the only countries in the world that doesn't have paid maternity leave. Our politics have skewed so far to the right in this country that these common-sense answers to problems in our society sound alien, but the outcomes as to how they are working in other countries is proof that they work.

Why do you think we've skewed so far to the right as a society or view these progressive ideals as so far left?

L: There are two reasons. One, our democracy is not a proportional democracy. We have the Senate, which is completely non-proportional, and we have the Electoral College. The population of our country is not represented accurately by our leadership. The second thing is our leadership doesn't represent our population. They represent whoever is giving them money to run their campaigns. Countries that have a proportional democracy are those with parliamentary systems, for example. Our system wasn't set up to represent the people. It was set up to protect slave owners. So, two hundred fifty years later there is a problem. We don't have a difference between slave states and non-slave states anymore. If you live in a small state your vote counts way more than someone who lives in a large state. We really don't live in a democracy.

States don't have their own identity like they did in the beginning. People move states in modern time. You could be a Texan in Wisconsin. You could be a Montana resident in Florida. People just go where they're going to be able to support their family. It's not because that's the identity of their being. If a lifelong Texan was going to lose their job if they didn't go to New York, they would go there because that's how you get food on your table. We have a mobile society and our states don't necessarily need to have that safety that they had back in the day. That's my perspective.

Are you saying the federal government should supersede state rights?

L: Yes. I think there are a lot of issues where our federal gov-ernment needs to have consistent legislation across the country, especially when it comes to healthcare as a right and gun legislation. That does not work out when it's at the state level because we do not have border patrol at the state lines. You can't say, "I'm going to stop you from coming into California with your AK-47 because they're not allowed here."

There is nobody at the state line to do that. It has to be consistent across the country.

The only law that could be localized and that could still work would be Red Flag laws. For example, the shooter in El

Paso (who killed twenty-two people and injured twenty-four others at a Walmart on August 3, 2019) came from my area in Texas. He had purchased his weapon online. We could have investigated that man and potentially prevented that tragedy, but legally the state of Texas won't allow our city to pass a Red Flag law. In order for that to happen, it would have to come from the federal government or we would have to flip our state legislature—either one of those things, I'd be fine with.

What do you think about leaving public school education to states?

L: It's very difficult to standardize education by legislation because the problem is each community has different issues. In a poor community, no matter how much you legislate those kids are not going to have the opportunities that kids in a wealthy community have. Even if you could clone schools and teachers everywhere, parents are going to go out and give their kids extra tutoring and exposure to more things. Education is really difficult. I can see a standard minimum would be useful though. I'm not against a standardized minimum like the Common Core concept, where at least it says, "You're going to learn at least this."

Do you have ambitions to run for higher office?

L: We'll see. Right now things are at such a tipping point both in the country and in Texas that I have to see where things are going. We just passed term limits for our city. Our mayor has served twenty-six years, but being the mayor is really a volunteer job. They get paid five hundred dollars per month.

Maybe someday I'll see about going to the Texas State House. It's going to depend on this next year and whether we're able to flip our state House and have control over the redistricting process. They will be redistricting in 2021. Right now there is Republican control of the executive branch and in both Houses. They have been given the go ahead by the Supreme Court to do whatever they want. Gerrymandering is basically an open option now. We are very gerrymandered right now. The Republicans will do whatever they can to stay in power. It is possible to flip the state House—we have to flip nine seats.

The Democratic Party and a lot of other organizations are very focused on Texas. If we could flip the House we could potentially keep that gerrymandering to a minimum, and then I would have a shot at running for higher office.

JS: Lauren said she is proud that her two young sons get to see her as a city councilwoman.

L: It's good for them to see their mother do something that's not just for them. It also models being a contributor to society to them.

What are the most pressing issues you're trying to keep or achieve?

L: Politically there are a couple of things on my agenda. I would like to see our city be a local leader for environmental policy. We have a good reputation in the North Texas area for environmental policy, but I think we're still far behind where we could be. I'd like to push that and potentially have a climate action plan in our city. Dallas is doing that right now.

I'm also working on getting more diversity and inclusion initiatives by making sure our city is celebrating everyone who lives here. We have a huge south Asian population, an east Asian population, a significant Hispanic and black population, an LGBTQ population, and we're not recognizing everyone so

241

I'm working on that.

With all of these things, I'm doing my best and I'm hoping to make some headway.

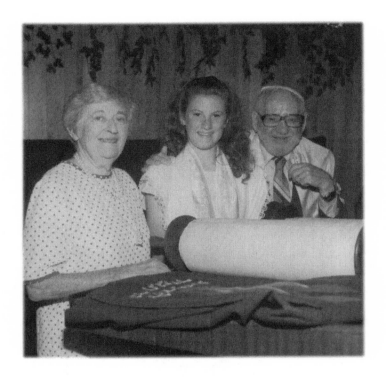

Lauren and Her Grandparents

Book Club Questions

Whose political shaping story resonated with you the most?

Not everyone in the book fits easily into a political party "box." What do you think about that?

Are there any stories that swayed you in any way to consider an alternate political point of view?

What is your political shaping story?

About the Author

Julie Samrick is passionate about telling stories that capture the human experience. She is also the author of *Murphy's Miracle: One Dog's Wild Journey*, which was inspired by a true story that happened in her community.

Julie lives in Northern California with her husband and their four children. She holds a degree in English from the University of California, Berkeley.

You can connect with Julie and learn more about her work at www.JulieSamrick.com.

Made in the USA
Columbia, SC
15 September 2020